GW01316430

Finding the Yes in the Mess

—⁀⁀⁀—

Stephen Critchlow

xulon
PRESS

Finding the Yes in the Mess
by Stephen Critchlow

Printed in the United States of America

ISBN 978-1-60266-110-3

www.xulonpress.com

Contents

—ᨸᨸ—

Foreword

—ꝼꝼꝼ—

This is an important, very readable, timely contribution which tackles the problem of suffering. We can be very grateful to Dr Critchlow for his courageous and insightful thoughts which will help the ordinary Christian as well as the scholar to reassess inadequate time-worn solutions to this painful issue. Many are still unconvinced by traditional clichés which are meant to clothe this subject with public acceptability. Dr Critchlow will not serve you with such, but will offer many fresh lines of inquiry which may prove fruitful for those still grieving in their own pains and those of others, and are wanting deeper understanding.

This book is concerned with the issue of theodicy, the justice of God. How is it that God's almightiness does not prevent or interfere with areas of pain, into which we would act if we had the ability? Does a loving God really care or is he not almighty? Most of us wish to keep the first description of God, which is a biblical description – God is love. He really is loving and caring. However also, we don't wish to let go of the second, that God is almighty and so is still in control. Such is somehow comforting. There is a security in this latter assertion making us feel that the universe won't run away with us. However we will find from Dr Critchlow's book that Jesus did not take this simplistic latter view of a fully controlled universe as much as tradition would seem to have it so.

Looking at a field of wheat spoiled by disorderly tares Jesus says, "An enemy has done this." He parabolically is referring to the apparent confusion which exists in God's Kingdom. The Kingdom is God's reigning and getting his will done on earth. (Matt 6:10, 13:28) It is a God-job of huge dimensions getting God's will done in a universe such as ours. Dr Critchlow's insights are helping us to dig deeply into God's revelation.

Both non-believers who have not been convinced by traditional answers, and Christians, who are not satisfied by shallow ones, but still are trusting Jesus and a loving God, will find this book rewarding for the seeds that will be planted in our hearts which with time bring a harvest of understanding of what the Bible does say on this topic.

However there are at least two other features which I would commend about "Finding the Yes in the Mess." One is the large number of anecdotes, pithy sayings and quotations which make this book such a delightful read. Here you will find a mine of appropriate illustrations. The second is the trained mind of an experienced Christian psychiatrist who reflects the mind of Jesus, who is the Wonderful Counsellor (Isaiah 9:6), whom you will meet in these pages. Dr Critchlow has had a long career in applying truth, thoughtfully, to himself and to large numbers of needy and hurting people, people who need the love which he manifests as well as the empathy he is able to sensitively exude in opening up the mysteries of the human heart.

I'm pleased and honoured to commend this book. While I may have expressed some things differently as I continue to seek out the truth, nevertheless I know my thinking has been enhanced in many areas by Stephen Critchlow's thoughts and words. He writes as a friend wanting to reach our real needs. For me he is a friend of nearly thirty years and whose professional and theological judgements I respect. There is much need for work to be done in these areas of thought, experience and revelation. Stephen has made a great contribution. I commend him and his pages of concentrated and distilled wisdom to you. May God who is light and Jesus, the Light of the World bring more light yet onto this subject by the entrance of these words.

R.T. Forster 2005

Introduction

—〰—

"How can you expect me to believe in a God of love when all I seem to experience is pain and heartache?" This is a valid question that demands real answers.

The world itself is in a mess. Can there be a "yes" in the mess? What or who causes the mess, and in this messed-up world are there any real answers?

In our personal lives, the worst pain is often internal and related to past problems. Is there any way to be free from the past?

In this book I have attempted to address these issues.

In writing this book I wish to express my sincere thanks to Dr and Mrs Jim Ferguson, Dr Linda Van Wyk, Mrs Anne Williamson, and Pastor Ray Mayhew for their very helpful comments on the first draft. I appreciate the excellent teaching I have received from the Ichthus Christian Fellowship in London over the years, and particularly from Roger Forster. This has been fundamental in shaping my thinking. I am very grateful for his foreword to this book. I owe an immense debt to Richard Kimber who checked the final draft. I would also like to thank my dear wife Ros, who encouraged me to keep going. Her recent question to me however took me aback. "Why," she asked me, "are you writing a book on suffering this year, when we are celebrating our twenty-fifth wedding anniversary?" I was left speechless!

CHAPTER 1

THE WORLD IN A MESS

—٦٦٦—

If we could shrink the earth's population to a village of exactly one hundred people with everything else kept the same then this is how it would appear.

There would be 57 Asians, 21 Europeans, 14 from all of the Western Hemisphere and 8 Africans.

48 would be male and 52 would be female.

70 would be non-white and 30 would be white.

70 would be non-Christian and 30 would be Christian, at least in name.

6 people would own almost 60 per cent of the whole world's wealth and all 6 would be from the United States of America.

80 would have inadequate housing. 70 would not be able to read.

50 would be suffering from some form of malnutrition. One would be close to death and one would be about to be born.

48 would be unable to attend a religious meeting without fear of arrest or harassment or worse.

Only one would have had a college education.

One would own a computer.

Simply shrinking the world to a hundred people graphically describes what is going on in the world. The staggering needs of the world quickly become apparent. G K Chesterton has said, "Not only are we all in the same boat, but we are all seasick." In trying to understand the world's problems, we are faced with a major difficulty, but we can only see it from our own perspective. Monica Furlong, an English feminist writer, has stated, "I feel that the human condition is rather like being a fly crawling slowly over a huge and complicated pattern on the wallpaper and trying, from this point of disadvantage yet also of immediate experience, to calculate the appearance of the whole."

We may feel rather like Alexander the Great, described by Harold Lamb in his book, Alexander of

Macedon: The Journey to World's End. He describes memorably the consternation which came upon the Greek army following Alexander across Asia Minor when they discovered that they had marched clear off the map. They were using Greek maps which showed only a part of Asia Minor. The rest was blank space. In the rapid change seen in the twentieth and in the beginning of the twenty-first century, we may feel like the soldiers of Alexander, right off the map!

One way of coping with insurmountable problems is simply to ignore them and hope they will go away. In 1940 Captain Luis Conterno, a pilot from Peru, was forced to make an emergency landing in the mountainous interior of Peru. Instead of meeting hostile tribes as he anticipated, he met friendly people with white skin who greeted him in pure Castilian Spanish. How had they come to be there? In 1904 two families became lost while crossing the Andes from Peru to Brazil. They decided to remain in the mountains. The people whom the pilot met belonged to a group of 450 who were the descendants of these two families. For 36 years they had had no idea about what was happening in the outside world. The pilot told them many things they did not know. He talked about the two world wars, stock market crashes and the many other changes that had taken place. These seemingly lost people realised how fortunate they had been in avoiding being involved in these events. They expressed no interest in returning to so-called civilisation.

One quite understands that point of view. It would be easy to bury our heads in the sand and seek to forget the tragedies and difficulties of modern existence. However such is not an adequate response. Somehow we must try to understand the problems and find ways through them. Then we will be able to find some kind of hope for those caught up in devastating events, pains and fears which seem incomprehensible.

Western society has changed beyond recognition in the last 50 years. It is hard to understand how all these changes have occurred. There has been, for example, a subtle change in the way we apportion responsibility and blame. In Britain today we are part of a "victim culture." Instead of taking responsibility for our own actions and their consequences we are now encouraged from every quarter to see ourselves as victims at the hands of another. If one is unfortunate enough to burn oneself by holding a scalding cup of coffee between the legs whilst driving on the motorway, then the fault lies in the cup of coffee not carrying a warning on it to state that it is hot and might burn. We are much less able to face up to our own mistakes and to take responsibility for them. It always has to be someone else's fault and we are the innocent victims.

A second change in Western society has been our loss of sense of shame. Reality television has become a way of sharing one's worst attributes with the world. Fame matters and shame seems to no longer exist. The question hangs in the air as to what has changed so drastically in Western culture to cause this profound alteration in value systems. Many are left with a sense of deep confusion about these changes in our way of life. Personal dignity and honour are fading virtues. "Where is the sense in this mess?" many ask.

We have changed in our approach to children. We might say that we are a child-centred society, but in practice this is not borne out. In the seeming endless pursuit of material gain, children become of secondary importance. They are often seen as unwelcome intrusions in the lives of adults. The Mental Health Foundation report The Big Picture (1999), comments, "Our adult-centred society has tried to contain and limit the impact of children on adult life by either excluding them from much of it, blaming them for disturbing it, or by admitting them only as designer accessories, or treating them like pampered pets."

The high divorce rate is directly damaging to children. Children of divorced parents are twice as likely to experience psychological, economic and social problems in adolescence than are children of parents who stay together. That is the conclusion of a summary of over 200 studies carried out by the Joseph Rowntree Foundation. Other studies have shown that children from broken homes or born to unmarried mothers are much more likely to be abused than ones whose natural parents are married.

Drug abuse and the crime that accompanies it have reached epidemic proportions. Faced with the societal decay we can observe in Britain, we may readily feel tempted to go and join the families who were cut off in the mountains of Peru. Malcolm Muggeridge has said, "Western society is now in an advanced state of decomposition."

In the developing world the problems are rather different. The disparity between the "haves" and the "have nots" continues to widen. The problems of the West may be seen as people struggling to find their identity and place in a rapidly changing and confusing world. The problems in the developing world are more focused on how to survive. There is immense inequity in the world. The statistics are daunting. The share of the poorest fifth of the world population in global income has dropped from 2.3 per cent to 1.4 per cent over the last ten years. The proportion taken by the richest fifth on the other hand has risen from 70 to 85 per cent. In sub-Saharan Africa, twenty countries have lower incomes now in real terms than they did two decades ago.

In many less developed countries safety and environmental regulations are almost non-existent. Some trans-national companies sell goods in these already disadvantaged countries which are controlled or banned in the West. These include poor quality medical drugs, destructive pesticides or high tar and nicotine content cigarettes. As one writer put it recently, "Rather than a global village, this is more like global pillage."

I read a letter recently from someone who had visited Ghana. The sugar on the table was imported from France because French sugar from sugar beet was cheaper in Ghana than the more cheaply produced local sugar from sugar cane. This is all because of agricultural subsidies in Europe. That is global pillage.

Globalization and reducing the world to a global village has not been beneficial for most people in the Third World. As M De l'Engle, a North American author said, "Half the world is starving and half is on a diet."

A recent survey in the British Medical Journal reports that in South Asia where a quarter of the world population lives, half the population lives below the poverty line. Some 34 per cent of the world's child deaths occur in this region which has almost two thirds of the global burden of malnutrition. Of the nearly four million child deaths each year, over two thirds are attributable to infection. In the United States, annual health expenditure per person is around $4,000. In Nepal, on the other hand, the government outlay is just three dollars for each person and in India, Pakistan and Afghanistan it is only slightly better at four dollars per person.

Man's Mess

On Tuesday, 5 September 2002 Mr Kakani, the chief nurse in the intensive care ward at Nyankunde Christian hospital in the Democratic Republic of Congo, had just finished early morning rounds. He was on the point of going to the morning praise service when he heard gunshots and screaming. Seven thousand soldiers were rushing towards the hospital. With their faces painted and carrying rifles and bayonets, machetes and knives they started to kill everyone whom they found in their way. These soldiers from the Ngiti tribe hated the people from the Hema tribe, and had no love for the Christian hospital, which had a tradition of treating people with respect and dignity no matter what their faith or background.

Government soldiers sent to protect the Christian hospital fled when they saw the ferocity of the attack. A thousand people died in the first hours of the onslaught. The soldiers went through the 250-bed teaching hospital killing any patient who resembled a member of the Hema tribe. They were killed on the beds where they lay – children, adults, the elderly, women in labour and those with newborn babies. All were killed indiscriminately. After the massacre in the hospital, soldiers then went from house to house looking for anyone from the Hema tribe, often slitting their throats and throwing their bodies outside on the ground, women and children alike. The homes were then pillaged and burned to the ground. Others were beaten and tortured including Mr Kakani.

The hospital was then taken apart section by section, doors and windows, tables, chairs and equipment – everything was removed. All the books used for teaching and medical records were thrown onto a large fire. Hundreds of corpses were gathered during the fourth and fifth days and added to the flames. The remaining staff knew they had to leave. In the early morning of 12 September, in the pouring rain while soldiers were sleeping or still looting distant homes, over 1,200 hospital staff and mission personnel quietly departed. After living off rainwater and sugar cane in the jungle for several days, they finally arrived exhausted at Oicha Christian Hospital on 22 September.

If we are to have any proper view of God and his love and understanding of suffering, then the conclusions we reach must be adequate to deal and cope with such tragedies as these. Because these events happened in Africa they are not common knowledge. Everyone knows what happened on what has been called simply 9/11 in New York, USA, but tragedies such as these from Africa are not widely reported. The Western media are primarily interested in broadcasting news items of interest to the West.

In another fearsome atrocity, 800,000 were killed in Rwanda in 1994 in just over 100 days. The suffering of the Rwandan people has been immense. It is still difficult to imagine what caused those killers to perpetrate such a blood bath. Many of those involved could not understand later how they had acted in the way that they did. They felt taken over by other forces. A blood lust entered into them. Many of those who survived had endured rape, torture or mutilation. The psychological traumas experienced will remain with many for the rest of their lives. The news moves on from Rwanda, but the scars and the broken lives remain.

Faced with recent atrocities and the gnawing anxiety that follows, many will ask, "Can I still believe in a God of love? Could God not have intervened to prevent tragedies like these?" The pain and suffering of the individuals involved is intense. Lives are damaged almost beyond repair. Where can the resources be found to deal with such physical and emotional needs? Can any theology or philosophy begin to address such damage, pain and loss? In what ways can the fear be alleviated? There is a tremendous need for physical and psychological help for lives that are shattered by these atrocities, and the panic and anxiety that may follow. Some may be able to find a pathway through their suffering. For many others there is a great need for healing from the traumas and terrors they have experienced.

Genetic Mess

Before training in psychiatry I spent some years in paediatrics. One of the more challenging aspects to the job was to look after children with inherited illnesses. Several of these are caused by chromosomal abnormalities. One such condition is Edward's Syndrome. I remember one small boy born with this condition. He was a pathetic little being with misplaced ears and a long narrow head. His brain was underdeveloped and he needed artificial breathing apparatus to keep alive. It was very difficult to explain to the parents that this little one really had no hope of survival and it would be better that the breathing apparatus should be removed and the infant allowed to die a natural death. These kinds of decisions are among the most difficult a doctor ever has to take. There is of course a world of difference between the removal of artificial means used to sustain life and the purposeful shortening of life by a definite action. One allows a natural death to occur, the other is euthanasia. Most doctors accept the need for the first, whilst being strongly opposed to the second. Sometimes parents may be reluctant to contemplate the inevitable and may wish the doctor to prolong life by all means, but this can be unjustified when faced with a terminal condition, and no evidence of any quality of life.

Any discussion of the problem of suffering needs to address questions such as, "How do you account for inherited deformities and genetic diseases?" "How can God be a God of love and allow these conditions in the human race?" Tough questions. Are there any answers?

Down's Syndrome is another example of a condition caused by an extra chromosome. With this condition the appearance is quite typical and the head is smaller than normal. Down's Syndrome individuals have lower intelligence than normal, with an IQ varying between 20 and 75. They are usually very warm and friendly. Some may have other medical conditions in addition and their life span is shorter than usual. Many may be capable of simple work when they become adults. Near our previous home in Belfast is a cafeteria which employs Down's Syndrome young people. They take simple orders, help prepare and serve the food and are happy and fulfilled in these occupations. Most will continue to require some kind of supportive environment throughout life.

Here is what a child with Down's Syndrome has said. "Hello! I'm Orlana ... What you might not be able to tell is that I can speak all sorts of languages like Hebrew (my Bar-Mitzvah was wonderful), Italian, Spanish, German, Greek and a little Japanese." She plans to go to a college that specializes in independent living. She goes on to explain that she was born with

Down's Syndrome, which means that she has one more chromosome than others in each one of her cells. This chromosome, she is pleased to say, makes her "special" in lots of different ways. She explains that this means she is very nice and everyone seems to really like her and then talks about her hopes to learn to cook and ride on buses. She is glad that people read about her and explains that people with Down's Syndrome have more in common with most people than differences from them.

They are able to appreciate the emotional side of life and add a lot to the lives of those around them. After our church service recently a new baby was brought in by her parents. It was touching to see the evident joy it gave a teenager in our church with Down's to hold the baby for a few moments. Besides giving a lot of joy to those around them and enjoying life themselves, Down's adolescents and adults are often very intuitive and perceptive to spiritual realities.

It is not easy however to cope with all aspects of Down's Syndrome. Friends of ours in Cyprus have two children with this chromosomal abnormality. One boy, Solomon, is their own and they have adopted another son. It was a courageous decision for them to welcome this second child into their home and it has not been easy for them, particularly since their own son has had a lot of physical problems. When I was in Cyprus recently it was thrilling to see Solomon's genuine love for Christ and others. He prayed for me before I left and this meant a lot to me.

Many genetic conditions are obvious at birth, but there are a few that show no signs till later on. This can be even more difficult to cope with. Huntington's Chorea is one of these conditions. It often does not show itself before adult life, and at this stage many will have borne children and passed the illness on to their offspring. It is a severe and fatal illness. There is progressive loss of muscle tissue with abnormal movements. The ability to walk and move is gradually lost, and ability to carry out normal bodily functions deteriorates. Along with this there are mental health problems. Depression is common and suicide is a distinct possibility. Increasing confusion and dementia often occur. It is not easy for relatives and professional staff to observe this progressive and insidious decline. It is perhaps even more difficult for those who know they already have the disease in a latent form. Scott Porter described what it was like to have Huntington's Chorea in the book Blue Institution.

He was institutionalized at the age of twenty. Scott states that Huntington's Chorea is "one of Mother Nature's cruellest jokes." Huntington's Chorea has rendered Scott virtually unable to do anything for himself. He is unable to communicate verbally. He can only communicate using subtle vibrations. His brilliant mind is still intact but his body no longer wants to function. It is a tragedy.

These are his anguished words spoken from a trapped body. "Sometimes I feel depressed. I mean they shoot horses don't they? I'm in a body that doesn't want to function properly any longer. Huntington's Chorea they call it. My father had it. Now I have it. It killed my father and it will surely kill me." He goes on to discuss the way the disease is slowly killing him, and robbing him of the ability to enjoy any quality of life. His anger and frustration are very obvious in his writing.

It is the "Why" questions which surface, that add to the pain. "Why me?" "What have I done to deserve this?" Diseases like Huntington's Chorea, where someone who has been well previously and then develops an insidious, crippling and terminal illness in adult life, lead to all kinds of questions about a God of love.

Other situations people find difficult have to do with the death of a close relative or friend, particularly when the death seems premature. Just recently I attended the funeral of a college friend who died at the age of 54 from cancer. He leaves a wife, two grown-up children and a son-in-law. It was hard to see him go. The funeral was packed and people had come from far and wide to pay their final respects. He had given over 20 years of his life to a painstaking translation project, which had been successfully completed a short time before his death.

I had known him very well and we had enjoyed a lot of good times together. Although he had accomplished many of his goals, it was not easy to see him go at such a relatively young age. Death is so painful, not just through the loss itself, but through the many questions that remain. As a psychiatrist working with the elderly, the pain of the loss of a spouse seems very hard to bear, and the grief, pain, restlessness and depression may last for a long time, sometimes years.

In trying to come to terms with inherited diseases and death whether premature or not, many will be troubled by the question, "Why does God allow such pain and suffering?" This question will need proper answers. Pious platitudes won't help here!

CHAPTER 2

CAN THERE BE A YES IN THE MESS?

—ɯ—

The North Wind and the sun were arguing as to which was the more powerful and agreed that the victor would be the one who could cause a traveller to take off his outer clothes. The North Wind tried first and blew with all his power. But the more he blew, the closer the traveller wrapped his cloak around him. In the end the wind abandoned the attempt and asked the sun what it could do. The sun just gently shone. As soon as the traveller felt the rays of the sun, he took off one piece of clothing after another, and finally went for a swim in a stream.

This story by Aesop shows that persuasion is better than force. Love is like the sun shining. As we feel the warmth of the sun and readily shed some clothing, so with love. As we appreciate that we are loved, cared for and important so we find it easier to open out and share of ourselves. Love is power. It is the greatest power.

Sometimes through difficulties in life we find it difficult to share of ourselves. There are hindrances and obstacles to our being real with other people. The gentle, healing stream of love, however, can undo the pain and turmoil of the past.

For me, one of the best illustrations of the power of love is the story of Father Damien. He was born in Belgium in 1840 and initially worked in Hawaii, where leprosy had become widespread. The government purchased property on an island, called Molokai and established a settlement where those who had leprosy could be segregated from the rest of the population. In 1860, 141 lepers were taken to the island of Molokai. They had no houses, no provisions and no doctor or priest. They felt hopeless, cut off from their loved ones and abandoned to die. Molokai became a word filled with dread. A petition was sent to the bishop for a priest to be sent on a yearly basis. Damien was the first to volunteer. At this stage 800 lepers were in the settlement on the island with afflicted lepers continuing to arrive by boatloads.

Father Damien vigorously tackled every need the lepers had. He cleaned wounds, bandaged ulcers, and even amputated gangrenous limbs. On first coming to the island, he was careful to take precautions against the disease. But he lived among his people, tending their sores and sharing their food. He didn't hold back from embracing the lepers as his own brothers and sisters. This is just as Jesus did. Mark 1:41 says, "and moved with compassion he stretched out his hand, and touched him." Damien followed this example. By 1885, eleven years after going to the island, it became clear that Father Damien too had leprosy. He addressed his congregation as "Brethren and fellow lepers."

Over the next five years he carried on caring for his fellow lepers. The disease gradually took over his body and he became horribly disfigured. His hands and feet were crusted with sores but he worked tirelessly and with great courage until three weeks before his death. It was during Damien's years on the island that a Norwegian doctor, Gerhard Hansen, first identified the bacillus of leprosy.

The author Robert Louis Stevenson was very affected by the work of Father Damien. He visited Molokai shortly after Damien's death and found "abominable deformations of our common manhood. A population as only now and then surrounds us in the horror of a nightmare. The butt ends of human beings lying there almost unrecognizable but still breathing, still thinking, still remembering. A pitiful place to visit, a hell to dwell in." Stevenson became friendly with those who worked on the island and mixed freely with the lepers and played with the children. At this stage Stevenson himself was suffering from tuberculosis. What he saw on the island made a dramatic impact upon him. Before leaving the island Stevenson composed a poem to the nuns who worked with the lepers. This was addressed to the Reverend Sister Marianne;

Matron of the bishop home, Kaluapapa,
To see the infinite pity of this place,
The mangled limbs, the devastated face,
The innocent sufferers smiling at the rod,
A fool were tempted to deny his God.
He sees, and shrinks; but if he looks again,
Lo, beauty springing from the breasts of pain!
He marks the sisters on the painful shores,
And even a fool is silent, and adores.

The story of Father Damien shows that love is prepared to make the ultimate sacrifice. Love brings tremendous power to change the lot of one's fellow man. Stevenson's reaction is interesting. At first he is so overpowered by the suffering that he is tempted to write God off as the perpetrator of some monstrous calamity. Later as he reflects on the compassion shown by the nuns, he sees a greater power at work and that is the power of love. There is something greater than suffering and that is love itself.

I was impressed recently by reading the story of another man, Dr Aniru Conteh who died recently of Lassa fever. He was a world expert on the disease and had worked with the deadly virus for many years. Lassa fever takes its name from a small village in Nigeria, where a mysterious outbreak in a mission hospital in 1969 led to the death of two nurses.

Aniru Conteh joined the team working on Lassa fever in 1979. During ten years of civil war in Sierra Leone in the 1990s and instability in West Africa, he worked skilfully and courageously to keep running a programme to control Lassa fever. In spite of funding difficulties, low staff numbers, civil unrest, corruption and violations of human rights, he continued in his work. His family took refugees into their home frequently, and his example was an inspiration to many others to provide homes for those fleeing persecution and civil war. On 17 March 2004, while treating a patient, Dr Conteh unfortunately pricked himself with a needle and became infected with the Lassa virus. He died of the disease that he had spent his life seeking to control. In the face of suffering he had refused to give up and finished by paying the ultimate sacrifice. He demonstrated a willingness to be involved with humanity no matter how great their needs. There is power in this kind of love. It overcomes the pain and obstacles and is willing, if necessary, to pay the ultimate price.

One of the reasons we fail to act in love is because we imagine we can do so little. It becomes easier to turn off the television, ignore the repeated calls on the radio or appeals through the post from the many charities that seek to claim our sponsorship. We become overwhelmed and the temptation is to do nothing. But the little we can do can transform.

Jesus told the story of a poor widow who put just a small coin in the offertory at the temple. Jesus commends this poor widow because although to the outsider it seemed a very small gift, it was actually all she had. It represented a much greater sacrifice than the larger offerings of the rich. (Luke 21:1-4)

A similar sacrifice was made by one of the explorers on Shackleton's expedition to the North Pole. Sir Ernest Shackleton was asked to talk about his most terrible moment in the Arctic. He told the story of one night when they had given out the last ration of the biscuits – one each. There was nothing else left. When it seemed that everyone was asleep, Shackleton sensed a stealthy movement and saw one of the men turning around to see how the others were getting on. Thinking everyone was asleep, this man stretched over to the next sleeping man, took his biscuit bag and removed the biscuit. Shackleton found it difficult to believe what he was seeing. He would have trusted his very life in the hands of this man! He wondered whether in the end he was turning out to be a thief in these tragic circumstances. Was he stealing the man's last biscuit?

Then Shackleton saw something else. He observed the man take the biscuit out of his own bag and then put both biscuits back into the bag at the sleeping man's side. Shackleton said, "I dare not tell you that man's name. I felt that act was a secret between himself and God." The widow's mite and the man's biscuit, although small by themselves, represented huge sacrifices. This is the kind of love that changes the world.

Sometimes those that made the sacrifice are remembered, sometimes not. As light seems much brighter when all around is dark, so small acts of love shine brightly in the midst of suffering. As John states, "The light shines in the darkness and the darkness has not overcome it." (John 1:5 RSV) Suffering can be overcome by love. Suffering may seem difficult to understand and we may feel tempted to abandon the attempt. Sacrificial love when it meets that suffering is equally hard to explain. We will need to examine both in seeking to address the problems that we face in today's world.

If you asked the man in the street about selfless love, he would probably begin to talk about one, Agnes Gonxha Bojaxhiu who was born on 26 August 1910 in Skopje, Macedonia. Most of us know her as Mother Teresa. In 1952 she opened the first home for those dying on the streets of Calcutta. Since then her Missionaries of Charity have grown from twelve, to thousands of people ministering to the poorest of the poor in 450 centres around the world. She has opened homes for the dying and unwanted from Calcutta to New York to Albania. She was in the forefront in establishing homes for AIDS victims.

For over 45 years Mother Teresa looked after the poor and the dying and the unwanted all over the world. She said, "At the end of our lives we will not be judged by how many diplomas we've received, how much money we have made, or how many great things we have done. We'll be judged by the statement, 'I was hungry, and you gave me to eat. I was naked, and you clothed me. I was homeless and you took me in.'" (Matthew 25:35)

Mother Teresa met the real needs of people. The physical needs were always there but she knew, as well, how to touch the heart and soul of the person to bring him or her back into relationship with others and with God himself. Mother Teresa is known across the world for her dedication to the poorest of the poor. In the life of Mother Teresa we see genuine love because love is seen by what it does.

One of the key statements in the Bible is found in 1 John 4:8, where it simply states, "The one who does not love does not know God, for God is love." The test of our genuine love for God is seen in our love for others. God's nature is love. When John states "God is love" what does this mean? It is saying that God has limited himself to act only in love. Love and love alone will guide his actions. Love is his very nature.

1 Corinthians 13 is often read at marriage ceremonies. Here is what it says in verse 13. "But now faith, hope, love abide, these three; but the greatest of these is love." It is a tragedy that years of Christian history seem to have forgotten and omitted this very basic concept. In the many credal statements of the early church the fact that God is love is omitted.

Ros and I have been happily married for twenty-five years and we are looking forward to celebrating our anniversary. One of the joys of married life is to be able to say with genuineness to the other "I love you." I think there are few days in our married lives that we have not said this to each other. If there were no actions to show that love, such statements might seem empty and meaningless. My wife might well expect that I would show my love to her in many different ways. This will involve spending time together, gifts and hugs and kisses. It may also involve getting rid of the leaves from the lawn in autumn! I have tried to explain to Ros, my wife, that this task is not strictly necessary and that the leaves on the lawn are doing it no harm. She fails to see my point of view. So I remove the leaves. Love keeps our marriage together.

There is a saying by St John of the Cross, a great saint of the Middle Ages, "In the evening of life, we will be examined in love." He also states, "Where there is no love, pour love in and you will draw love out."

Looking back over my life in years to come I want it to be known chiefly for its love. I have a long way to go! It is as we pour love in that we will draw love out. Those who have brought the greatest good to the world have been those with hearts burning with love. John the apostle clearly understood the meaning of love. It was he who had leant on the breast of Jesus at the last meal which Jesus had shared with his disciples. He could hear the heartbeat of Jesus and could pick up the whispers of the love that Jesus had for mankind. As is evident from his gospel and epistles, he was the disciple who really understood Jesus and his love better than the others. Small wonder then that at the empty tomb "he saw and believed." (John 20:8) Tradition has it that as a very old man he was wheeled or carried in to the Christian assembly and he would talk only about love. He would say, "Brothers, love one another." What a tragedy that this central theme has been watered down and devalued over the ensuing centuries.

General Booth, the founder of the Salvation Army, acted in compassion when faced with the massive problems of alcoholism in East London at the end of the nineteenth century. He understood that to get people free and keep them liberated required restructuring of their lives. He was extremely successful. The Nottingham Journal writes this about him:

"William Booth started out from Nottingham, largely self-educated, penniless, and practically friendless. He had one fixed idea. The whole of his effort and talent would be directed to the one purpose, saving the world. Like his predecessor Wesley, he took the whole world as his parish. So well did he succeed that, before he died, his name was known in practically every country of that parish, and his followers numbered in millions. He began with nothing, had no money, no powerful friends, only his golden voice, his passion and the vision of man reconciled to God."

As he preached outside The Blind Beggar Tavern in Mile End Road, East London, he said, "There is a heaven in East London for everyone – for everyone who will stop and think and look to Christ as a personal Saviour."

From the pub came a volley of jeers and oaths followed by a rotten egg. The preacher paused, egg running down his cheek, prayed and turned west towards Hammersmith and his lodgings. He made his way through savage fighting men, ragged match-sellers, orange women, and Irish flower girls dressed only in soiled petticoats with their bare feet covered in dirt; children with wolfish faces gobbling up decaying food left by the street market, and swaying blind drunks in tap-room doorways. He strode past crowded tenements and stinking alleys where the dregs of society were trapped in an endless treadmill of despair and the dark alleys near the docks, where the sick and dying lay side by side on bare boards of fireless rooms under tattered scraps of blanket.

He used to tour the streets with his army of volunteers to find the alcoholics and those with no hope. He would bring them into meetings where they would feel the love of Christ and the compassion of their fellow men. Those who had come out of a life of misery could identify easily with those who were trying for the first time to get out of their dreadful circumstances. He would then re-integrate these men into society giving them worth and value. They would be given jobs and occupations, often taking them away from their immediate surroundings either to a farm in the country or sometimes even abroad, to separate them from their previous surroundings and habits. As a result, lives were transformed on a massive scale. Towards the end of his life he was asked to what he attributed his success. With tears streaming down his cheeks he said simply, "God had of me all that there was to have."

The same can be said of Mother Teresa. Love is love, when it is seen in action. We need more General Booths and Mother Teresas so that the world can see once again that Christian love is genuine. So many people have been turned against the Christian faith, I believe, because they have had doctrine preached at them. But they have failed to see genuine love demonstrated by the Church.

Christ was full of love. He touched the leper. He embraced the poor. He was a friend to the outcast whether a hated tax collector or a prostitute. The weak were encouraged and the sick healed. Day after day he expended himself to the point of exhaustion in moving out with compassion to meet the needs of a lost and suffering humanity. Love is love, because it acts!

Love And Relationships

There were four bulls who had become great friends. They went everywhere together, ate together, and lay down to rest together. They always kept close to each other so that if there was danger in the air, they could all face it together. Now a lion was determined to have them, but he could never get at them whilst they were together. He could take on any one alone, but not all four of them at once. He used to lie in wait for his opportunity. When one of the bulls strayed behind the others while they grazed, he would sneak up and whisper that the other bulls had been saying unpleasant things about him. This happened so frequently, that at last the four friends became uneasy in each other's company. Each one thought the other three were plotting against him. Finally, no trust existed between them and they went off by themselves. Their bond of friendship was broken.

This was exactly what the lion wanted. One by one he killed them and had four good dinners. Aesop's story reminds us that love is seen in friendship. Love is not an entity by itself. Love can only be seen through relationships. Without love, individuals move apart or separate.

Without love, friendships become fractured and people feel lonely, isolated, and succumb to the problems of life. In modern society in Great Britain, loneliness and isolation are major problems. Around a quarter of the elderly live by themselves. Many have lost their close friends and relatives or their spouses. They often feel lonely and isolated. They no longer have the friendships that they used to have in the past.

Many suppose that the main needs of the elderly are physical in terms of food, warmth, safety, hygiene and clothing. It may be forgotten that the deeper needs are for relationship, friendship, self worth, value and a sense of belonging. In institutions and in hospitals these vitally important aspects of life may be sacrificed by concentrating mainly on the physical needs. But when these deeper needs are not met the person can feel cut off and isolated, which can lead in its turn to despondency or clinical depression. People need help to maintain their circle of friendships. It is very sad to find a patient on a ward who has no friends or relatives who visit. In addition the interests of a person and their spiritual needs are extremely important. Without this a person can become isolated and find life sad and meaningless.

People hunger for relationship and for the knowledge that they are loved and valued. Too easily we can end up relating to others as "It" rather than as "Thou" as the philosopher Martin Buber has described in his book I and Thou. Too easily I can be trapped into seeing my patients as a collection of "Its" who need treatment rather than as "Thous," each of great value and significance. Love, according to Buber, is where we have a subject-to-subject relationship rather than a subject-to-object relationship. The temptation is to treat people as objects rather than as real persons.

People need to be treated as individuals and not as means to an end.

Western culture in so many ways has become goal-centred rather than people-centred. The important goals become financial prosperity and success at work and in leisure activities. In seeking to achieve these goals the need for maintaining relationships can easily become lost. Other people can become means to our achieving our goals rather than being important in their own right. They become, in Buber's terms, objects rather than subjects. We can become driven by the clock and our goals, rather than being driven by compassion.

In Africa there is a saying, "In the West you have clocks but in Africa we have time." In Africa it is normal to spend time greeting someone properly and inquiring about his or her welfare and that of the family. There is time for relationships. In the West this is often neglected. My friend Sergio, who has come from Brazil to help in a local church, finds some of the cultural differences strange. In Brazil when you ask, "How are you?" you expect to hear in detail exactly how the person is. In Northern Ireland people would seem irritated and look at their watches when he began to answer this question properly! In the West, this important question has been debased into a common courtesy. We are often so goal orientated that we do not really want to know how the other person is. We need to recover the art of building and maintaining relationships or it can easily become lost.

Earthly bonds mirror heavenly relationships. When the Bible teaches us about God, it teaches us about God in relationship. The Trinity is God in living, dynamic interaction. In the Trinity, we see an affinity of love between three members who are all equal but with separate functions. The Father loves the Son. The Spirit does the will of the Son and the Father. There is a flow of life between the three. It would seem that there is discussion of plans together in the Trinity. For example, God says, "Let us make man in our image, according to our likeness." (Genesis 1:26)

Man is made in the likeness of God and his relationships can mirror something of the loving interactions within the Trinity. The constant flow of life between the three members of the Trinity is reflected to a degree when humanity expresses itself in close loving bonds. That is why it can be devastating when relationships break down. The flow of life and love becomes blocked up like a dam.

In the closeness between Jesus and his Father, Jesus says, "The Son can do nothing of himself, unless it is something he sees the Father doing." (John 5:19) In talking about receiving the Spirit of God, Jesus states, "If a man loves me, he will keep my word, and my father will love him, and we will come to him and make our home with him." (John 14:23) There is loving co-operation between the members of the Trinity as God brings blessing into our lives. In living organisms movement is a characteristic feature of life. It is the same with spiritual life. Flow and movement indicate life. Life and love are on the move in the heart of God. If we are responsive then we, too, will be caught up in the divine momentum.

An illustration of the life of the Trinity concerns a friend of mine called Tom. He is a wonderful guy, and has spent many years working hard for the kingdom of God. He has unusual ways of portraying truth! One of the most remarkable stories about him is the time he went to a certain country where it was forbidden to directly preach about Jesus. Tom has ways of overcoming difficulties and apparent impossibilities. If anything is difficult or seems impossible, then Tom enjoys the challenge of overcoming it with God's strength and help.

Tom had a bicycle, and on the handlebars he carried bags full of Bibles. In this particular country it was not possible for Tom to give out the Bibles directly. To overcome this difficulty, on his bicycle helmet he had emblazoned "Trinity Company." This country had high unemployment and many people would approach him as he stood outside factories, at street corners or at their work places. They would ask, "What is this company?" "Can we join it?" "We would like to work with you. Is that possible?" Tom would reply, "Well, it is a very important company. Actually it is the first company that ever existed. In fact, it is a very high company, higher than the highest skyscraper."

The person would be intrigued to know that such an important company existed, and would be even more anxious to find out whether work opportunities existed. They might ask, "How does one get a job?" or perhaps, "Can you find me a job, Mr Tom?" Tom would answer, "Well, to get a job in this company, you have to meet the three bosses. Now these three chiefs are quite amazing people. For example, they all think the same and act the same. They all agree. There is never any arguing between them. They are very committed to each other and really care about each other. There is tremendous unity in decision making."

"Where do I go to meet the bosses, Mr Tom?" Tom would then tell them, "First you must meet the father of the company. He's the number one. Then there is the son. He is very important and you have to meet him to get to the father. You also need to understand the spirit in the company that keeps them all together." By this stage some would begin to realize that Tom was speaking of an unusual company.

He would go on to explain how they could get into the company by coming to know God on a personal level. And then he would be delighted to give them the Scriptures. Unorthodox maybe, but very effective. Well done, Mr Tom! It was an effective way to communicate the Gospel and also a very interesting portrayal of the life and work of the Trinity.

The most famous story of St Patrick relates to the shamrock. It is believed that St Patrick used the three leaves of the shamrock as a picture of the Trinity. One life in one plant but with three leaves representing the three persons of the Trinity. Other examples have been used. Steam, water and ice are three different forms of the same compound. All these descriptions however, fall short of being able to express the full reality of the Trinity.

It is hard to relate these truths in easily understood language. How does one capture the life and power of three separate beings all with one common identity? All living and being as one, breathing life and love into the world.

The Father is the head of the Trinity and in him all things consist. The Son is the only begotten Son, constantly begotten of the Father. The Spirit pours the power and life of God into our lives. Christ comes down from the Father, is born of a virgin and lives an exemplary life full of love and power, and then lays down his life on the cross for us.

Here is love. "But God demonstrates his own love toward us, in that while we were yet sinners Christ died for us." (Romans 5:8) Love in relationship in the Trinity became love in action on the cross. Christ became the willing sacrifice to redeem a bruised and broken mankind which was out of harmony with God and at odds with itself.

God's Self Statement

During the Korean War the communists arrested a South Korean Christian civilian and they ordered him to be shot. But when the Young Communist leader learned that the prisoner was responsible for an orphanage caring for little children, he changed his mind and spared him and killed the Christian prisoner's 19-year-old son in his place. They shot him right in front of the father's eyes.

Later on in the war as the tide changed, that same Young Communist leader was arrested by United Nations armed forces, tried and sentenced to death. But before this could be carried out, the Korean Christian whose boy had been murdered came forward and pleaded for the life of his son's killer. He said that this communist leader was young and did not really know what he was doing. The Christian said, "Give him to me and I will train him." The United Nations forces granted the request and the father took the murderer of his son into his own home and looked after him. Today that same young man, a murderer and former communist officer, is a Christian pastor.

Bahram, the son of the Iranian Anglican Bishop, Hassan Barnaba Dehqani Tafti, was cruelly murdered. His father prayed, "O God, Bahram's blood has multiplied the fruit of the spring in the soil of our souls; so when his murderers stand before thee on the day of judgment remember the fruit of the spirit by which they have enriched our lives and forgive." This kind of love is not known outside the presence and power of Christ.

These stories speak of the way that love sets no limits at all on how far it will go. It is prepared to forgive the worst enemy. Love is not ashamed to make the ultimate sacrifice. Love wants to embrace the world. Hate tends to be narrow and focused on the object of hatred. Love seeks to fill the universe with its very nature. There is no extent to which love will not go in seeking to redeem, bless and forgive. Stories like these demonstrate the true nature of love in showing there is no sacrifice that love will not make for its friends, or even for its enemies.

Although love wants to embrace the world, it does set a boundary around the type of action it will perform. Parents set boundaries to bring discipline and order to the life of the child, with the aim of protecting the child from harm. But finally one hopes that the boundaries will become internal. Then the child will appreciate what future conduct is appropriate, and will be able to reflect back on what might have been damaging at an early age.

Love is a boundary by its very nature. It will act in one way, but it will not act in another way. Love will seek to up-build, but not to destroy. Love will seek the best result in a given situation. It ends up much more often in the win-win situation. People will be helped and solutions will be found. But in this, love itself will have kept within certain boundaries. By the action that is demonstrated, we can often tell whether that action was done in love or not. Not that this discernment is foolproof. There will be actions done in love that we may never fully understand, and others that seem to have been done in love, which have been guided by ulterior motives.

It would be interesting to conduct an opinion survey on whether the actions of famous or notorious people have been carried out with loving altruism or not. On a scale of one to ten how would the actions of public figures measure up? Most people faced with the choice would not find it difficult to put a Hitler or Stalin at one end and a Mother Teresa at the other.

There is a general moral sense, integral to human nature, which is able to give an opinion on whether an action is loving or whether it is not. We can say with reasonable precision love acts in this way, but it would not act in another way. The capacity for moral judgment is common to humanity. It may be warped at times and it may be misinformed, but it is still there and able to judge actions pretty well.

When we turn our attention to God we discover that he has defined himself by stating, "God is love." He will act in love, and he will only act in love. When we see an action that cannot be conceived of as loving, can we say God did it? The moral sense that we all have is able to differentiate, with a degree of accuracy, actions that are loving from those that are not.

If God has said that he is love and yet seems to act out of character, then there is a problem. We are faced with a dilemma. Can acts that seem unloving be carried out by a God of love? The usual response to this dilemma is to say, "This action seems wrong or evil, but because God did it, it must by definition be a loving act. We cannot understand, however, how God could do it. It does not seem to fit." We are unable to solve the problem and conclude that our deductions must be wrong. We end up throwing our minds out. Alternatively we can say, "This action is not loving. If God did it then we cannot follow this kind of God." We throw God out.

The third alternative is rarely explored. "This action is not done in love. God is love. Therefore God did not do this particular action." Following through this third alternative, we find a different source for the action. If we accept this last position then it releases us to explore the possibility that other forces may be operating in this world. These forces, I believe, are evil forces, and are discussed more fully later.

In 1 Corinthians chapter 13 love is the ultimate reality. Faith and hope are also important but they are not as important as love. The chapter goes on to define the things that love will not do. In verses 4-8 we read, "Love is patient, love is kind and is not jealous; love does not brag and is not arrogant, does not act unbecomingly; it does not seek its own, is not provoked, does not take into account a wrong suffered, does not rejoice in unrighteousness, but rejoices with the truth; bears all things, believes all things, hopes all things, endures all things. Love never fails." These are the qualities that we see in love, and God himself has defined himself by these very qualities.

Love by its nature is a boundary. It will only act in accordance with its nature. When the Bible states that God is love, this means that God is setting himself an ethical boundary that even he will not transgress. He will never act outside of the boundary of love.

In reflecting on the nature of love, and how it acts, one further question is worth posing. On a scale of one to ten regarding love, where would you put God, and where would you put Christ? It is my impression that most people would see Christ as perfectly loving and score him ten. Where would they put God? If they answered this from their theology they would have to give the same score, which is ten. If they answered with their heart however, according to their experiences of life and all its problems, what number would they give? Perhaps he qualifies for a five or six.

This illustrates that there seems to have crept into Western theology a difference in our understanding between God and Christ. Christ is seen as perfectly loving and the stories we read of him in the

Gospels emphasize his love to the unfortunate, the oppressed, the needy, the sick and dying. However when we view God, we see him in a different light. We imagine that the ills in the world are his fault. It appears to us that God is less loving in some way than Christ, who is perfect love. This cannot be. Jesus says of himself , "He who has seen me has seen the Father." (John 14:9)

Jesus is saying here, as well as in many other places, that he and the Father are the same. There is no difference between them. Each has the same attributes, the same character and the same love. In other words, as we look at Christ, we see a picture of God in human form. We cannot therefore come out with any conclusion that makes God and Christ to be different. If we conclude this in our minds, or even feel it in our hearts, then it means that there is a mistake somewhere in what we actually believe in the depths of our beings.

CHAPTER 3

LOVE IN FOUR DIMENSIONS

—⁂—

Mum's Fault Or Dad's?

One person I'm glad that I never had as a patient was the famous writer and hymn writer, William Cowper. At the age of 32 he passed through a great crisis in his life and tried to end his life by taking opium. Then he hired a horse-drawn cab telling the driver to take him to the Thames where he intended to throw himself in from the bridge. It turned out to be one of London's foggiest nights. They drove around for an hour without finding the chosen spot. Disgusted, he decided to get out and walk there. But he found, to his amazement, that he had gone in a full circle and was back at his own doorstep. The next morning he fell upon a knife, but the blade broke and his life was spared. He then tried to hang himself and was cut down unconscious, but still alive. It was in the midst of this storm in his life that he found the power of Christ to transform him and was able to write such words as this.

Ye fearful saints, fresh courage take,
The clouds you so much dread,
Are big with mercy, and shall break,
In blessings on your head.

Cowper suffered from mental instability, but also moments of tremendous brilliance. He struggled because of the loss of his mother when he was five years old. He had also been badly bullied at school. He suffered severely with depression but his friendship with the minister John Newton of "Amazing Grace" fame was a great help to him.

When we say "God is love", the English language cannot really capture all the fullness of the word "love". In the Greek language there are four words for love, which express different shades of meaning. C S Lewis has examined this fully in his book The Four Loves. If we are to understand the nature and fullness of God's love, and what difference we should see in the world as a result of God's intervention in it, then an exploration of the different words for love is important.

"Storge" is the Greek word used to refer to the affection shown between members of a family. Family love is incredibly important. The bonding process between child and parent particularly in the first two or three years of life is a vital process. If the child lives with a loving, nurturing parent, then it will learn to appreciate love, and a strong bonding process is set in motion. If this process does not occur, either through absence of the mother, or through the mother giving contradictory feedback to the growing infant, then this bonding process goes wrong. Children who miss out on this important bonding process find themselves at a disadvantage.

The failure to make a positive bond with the mother makes it more difficult to make future positive bonds. If there has been a bonding failure, trust and security will be affected. These difficulties can of course be overcome. Recognizing the problem that has occurred is helpful in understanding how to overcome it. Individuals affected by such bonding failure may need encouragement to reach out to others in friendship, for example, or they may need reassurance that they are truly loved and accepted within relationships. C S Lewis struggled because of the loss of his mother and wrote, "It was sea and islands now. Atlantis had sunk." Cowper's loss of his mother seriously affected his mental health.

A mother's love is important in healthy growth and progress. If the mother herself is not present, an adequate substitute must be found. There must be a "good enough mother" for a child to have normal emotional health. Mothers can have tremendous impact, not only through their example but also through their prayers. Susanna Wesley, mother of John and Charles Wesley, spent one hour each day shut up with God praying for them. The two sons brought revival to England.

Picture another mother. A poor, old, worn out woman with wispy, silver hair has tears flowing down her cheeks. Her hands are busy in a washtub. But as she works she is calling out to God in prayer for her son, John who had run away to sea. He had become a very wicked man. He became a slave himself for a period of time and then became a slave trader. This son was the John Newton we have just mentioned. When God took hold of Newton's life, he was mightily used of God to bring many to Christ. No one can know how much is accomplished by a mother's prayers.

Not too many think of this old washerwoman when they sing these words,

Amazing grace how sweet the sound
That saved a wretch like me.
I once was lost, but now am found,
Was blind, but now I see.

One of the major difficulties some people face is when a parent has treated them extremely badly. The insults and pains of childhood often lie unresolved, buried deep in the psyche. The child may have no-one to turn to or may just be unable to unburden himself. These hurts, if not dealt with, will almost always surface in some form in later life causing further difficulties. The hurts sustained in childhood affect the adult. The problems we have had as children may be hidden or repressed, but they will still be there. In my professional life I meet many people who have had major emotional pain in their lives because their fathers treated them very badly. Sometimes it is the mothers or others who have been at fault. These early wounds are deep and have helped mould the adult personality.

Break-up of family life causes immense problems to children. Divorce has become much easier over the last 30 or 40 years in the United Kingdom. The resulting scars left in the lives of children are seldom healed. Often the children themselves do not realize fully what is happening to them at the time. They may blame themselves for causing the break-up of the family. Deep hidden scars may be present and carried into adult life.

Loss of parents by death or divorce is a well-known factor contributing to depression. William Cowper carried the scars from his childhood experience of the loss of his mother. We can do the same. Later on in this book we will look at ways in which some of these scars may be healed.

Many of us as men have struggled in our lives, because we never heard, "Well done" from our fathers. Men of that generation were not taught to encourage or compliment their children. Many of them had lived through the last war and were damaged and hurt as a result. Display of emotion was often seen as weakness. The warm hug and the encouraging word were foreign to many. It was just not the done thing. Toughness was what counted. The importance of encouraging a child was often just not realized. The damage of not hearing, "Well done" can continue into adult life. There are different ways of responding to this lack of affirmation. Having missed out in childhood we may compensate by putting ourselves under pressure to achieve and to win the accolade of important people in our circle. Alternatively, we may withdraw from challenges, feeling that attempting to overcome them is pointless because of a feeling of lack of self-worth. We can feel doomed to failure, often quite inappropriately, because we never experienced that early affirmation. Whatever our varied experience of childhood, most of us will have scars of one kind or another which need healing. On the other hand family love, when present, keeps the family together, strong and united and can give a tremendous start in life.

God talks about his love for his family in very tender terms. He says "Yet it was I who taught Ephraim to walk, I took them up in my arms; but they did not know that I healed them. I led them with cords of compassion, with the bands of love." (Hosea 11:3-4 RSV)

God is here pictured as a tender and loving father leading a tiny child and teaching him to walk. That is his nature. He is not a God who is distant and far away. But that child he cared for and taught to walk, turned against him. In the same way as the heart of God as father was broken by his child's rebellion, so the heart of Hosea was broken by his wife's desertion and the mess in his family life which was no fault of his own. Hosea learned the pain and agony in the heart of God through the breakdown in his own family relationships.

One of the great difficulties that people have today in comprehending the fatherhood of God is because of the very poor earthly fathers that they may have had. By contrast the beauty of a relationship with God is that he likes to be called "Abba" or "Daddy." He can be a wonderful father to us. The good news is that despite the problems we may have had in the past whether lack of mother, or poor bonding, or poor family relationships, or scars given us through lack of encouragement, there is hope for healing.

Finding Real Friendship

A second type of love discussed by C S Lewis is that of friendship love or "Philia". This is the love that draws people together in friendship and causes them to face the same direction. There is the sense of comradeship of doing things together, and each enjoying the company of the other. Mutual sharing of successes and failures will occur and future goals will be discussed. Support will be there in times of trouble. Deep friendships are not easy to come by and need effort and energy to sustain but there is mutual benefit and each enriches the other. The person without friends is consequently a much poorer individual.

When I first went up to Fitzwilliam College, Cambridge, I did not find the transition from home to university life particularly easy. On my first day there I met a fellow medical student whom I knew slightly, having played lacrosse with him in inter-school competitions. Over the next few weeks I began to get to know him much better as we sat together in our first medical school classes. We began to talk about religious themes. I would share with him that I knew that I had eternal life because of my relationship with Christ and because of the Word of God, which promised me eternal life through faith in Christ. He had studied religious knowledge at school to advanced level but had no personal assurance of being accepted by God.

Even though I was going through a difficult time on a personal level, every day I prayed hard for my friend that he would come to find faith in Christ. I am not one who tends to hear clearly from God very often. However there came a Sunday morning in the second term of my time at Fitzwilliam College when, as I prayed, I very clearly heard God speaking to my spirit saying, "Your friend will be converted today." I went to collect him in the usual way to take him to the evening meeting, but to my consternation I could not find him. I went to the meeting anyway. As I reached the meeting I was thrilled to find my friend already there. He had given up waiting for me! At the end of the service I could not believe how rapidly he ran to the front of the church to give his life to Christ.

This was the beginning of an enduring friendship. Over the next two or three years in College and then at medical school in King's College Hospital, London, we did virtually everything together. We played sports, worked in the Christian Union, and went on mission together. We joined the Ichthus Christian Fellowship in London in 1977 and were much encouraged by the ministry of Roger Forster and others. Over the years our paths have separated to a degree as I spent several years in Cyprus; my friend spent many years in Israel.

True friendship is not easy to find and less easy to maintain. Sometimes distance places a strain on friendship that is hard to overcome. True friendship however is extremely important and its loss can have devastating results.

Betrayal of trust is dimly viewed and can cause the friendship to founder. Such a betrayal was felt in the "Night of the Long Knives" when the British Prime Minister, Harold Macmillan, sacked seven Cabinet colleagues. Jeremy Thorpe, MP, said regarding this, "Greater love hath no man than this that he lay down his friends for his life," famously misquoting the Bible. In this statement he was accusing Harold Macmillan of placing his own political career above his responsibilities to his friends.

Victor Hugo, on the other hand, was very much loved by the French people. In 1870 the Prussians had advanced and were threatening the very gates of Paris. Victor Hugo came in at the very last moment, on the very last train, just before the city was completely surrounded. On the way he had seen villages burning but he still came to voluntarily imprison himself within Paris. The people gave him a memorable welcome and they never forgot his voluntary sharing of their sufferings. Someone has said "A true friend comes in when everyone else goes out."

Henry Brooks Adams stated, "One friend in a lifetime is much; two are many; three are hardly possible." What he is referring to here is that true friendship involves deep mutual sharing in an atmosphere of trust. This needs time, patience and commitment that do not happen overnight. It is not easy to find this depth of sharing and if friendships are betrayed it becomes more difficult to reach out again. Every attempt to reach out involves becoming open and vulnerable. Following disappointment, many withdraw as they feel the risk of becoming open once again is not worthwhile.

I was recently involved in a church mission to Germany where we had many opportunities to speak particularly to young people. This was a thrilling occasion and many people gave their lives to Christ. Having shared on a Sunday morning in church, a girl came to me in a state of distress. As I talked to her further, it became apparent that the sudden moving away of two of her close friends during her teenage years had damaged her whole emotional life. She was still bearing the scars of loss of friendship.

One of the most astonishing stories of true friendship is that of Anne Sullivan and Helen Keller. Anne Sullivan had been born almost blind and was brought up in poverty. Her mother died and she went into the poorhouse. Later at the Perkins Institute for the Blind a brilliant operation brought back her sight. Following this she decided that her life's work would be the care of the blind.

In Alabama a girl was born, Helen Keller, who was destined to become famous although she could not see, speak or hear. Anne Sullivan began by patiently teaching Helen Keller 30 words within two weeks, spelling them by touching her hand. Through this steady, ongoing tuition Helen Keller learnt to communicate effectively and was even able to hold public lectures. For 49 years teacher and pupil remained inseparable. Then Anne Sullivan, now Mrs Macey, became blind again. Then it was Helen Keller who taught her how to overcome her blindness and she now taught her former teacher. Finally Helen Keller stood at the deathbed of her other half. When it was all over she recorded in her memories, "I prayed the strength to endure the silent dark until she smiles upon me again."

Helen Keller overcame suffering through the help of a lifelong friend. This is a poem she wrote.

> They took away what should have been
>   my eyes.
> (But I remembered Milton's Paradise.)
> They took away what should have been
>   my ears.
> (Beethoven came and wiped away my tears.)
> They took away what should have been my
>   tongue.
> (But I had talked with God when I was
>   young.)
> He would not let them take away my soul.
> (Possessing that, I still possess the whole.)

A similar story of tremendous sacrifice for a friend is the story of Albrecht Dürer. As a child he had always wanted to paint. He met a friend who had exactly the same idea and the two became roommates. Both being poor, they found it difficult to make a living and study at the same time. His friend offered to work manually while Dürer painted. Then when Dürer would begin to sell his paintings, his friend would have the chance to paint. Dürer agreed and worked at his art while his friend worked long hours to provide for them both. One day Dürer sold a woodcarving and the chance came for the roles to be reversed. However when his friend tried to paint he found that his hard manual work had stiffened and twisted his fingers so he could no longer paint well.

When Dürer learned what had happened to his friend, he was very upset. One day on returning home, he heard the voice of his friend and saw the gnarled hands pressed together in prayer in front of him. He knew the best way to show the world appreciation of his friend was by painting his hands as they were in prayer. Dürer painted The Praying Hands which are now famous and have been an inspiration to many.

"Faithful are the wounds of a friend." A true friend will not hesitate to speak the truth to us. Because of the friendship, we will often be able to receive the truth from that person whereas if someone else said the same thing to us we might not. Friendship grows by working together on projects. It has a side-by-side quality to it. It is facing the same direction together. It is a precious resource in life.

Lack of friends is often self-inflicted. I meet many old people who have paid little attention to their friendships and now have no-one to care for them in their old age. It is very sad to find some patients on my ward who have no visitors to see them. No-one seems interested in them and they feel rejected. Maybe they have not made the effort to maintain friendships. Perhaps their behaviour patterns have caused others to withdraw from them.

It is an immense sadness when people are totally isolated without a call from anyone that they can say is a friend. At other times people carry wounds deep within them caused by those whom they thought were friends but have turned out false.

God shows us the love of friendship. He says "No longer do I call you slaves ... but I have called you friends." (John 15:15) Abraham was called "the friend of God." (James 2:23) It is tremendous to know that the relationship between God and us is one of friendship. As we turn our lives over to God and his purposes then we can know his closeness. God's plans for us are not hard and difficult. When we enter into friendship with God we find we are facing in the same direction. His thoughts become our thoughts and his ways become our ways. We can listen to him. We can appreciate him as a true friend and with him as our true friend we can walk together in the joy of companionship. It is the greatest friendship that can ever be known.

Pure Eros

One of the most unusual meetings that led to a romantic attachment was that between Lauritz Melchoir, the Wagnerian tenor, and Maria Hacker a Bavarian actress. Lauritz was in the garden at his music school practising the line, "Come to me, my love, on the wings of light." Almost as soon as the words had escaped from his lips, something amazing happened. A young lady literally dropped out of the sky and landed at his feet. Maria had been doing a stunt for a film. As part of the act she parachuted out of a plane. The wind had changed direction and she changed course and landed in the garden. It was more than the wind that changed course that day! With such an auspicious start, how could they fail to start a relationship? Romance blossomed and they ended up marrying each other.

Thomas Edison the famous inventor was married but his wife died when he was 37 years old. He then met a girl called Mina, and taught her the Morse Code which he then used to send her a marriage proposal. She sent back her acceptance in code. Another unusual proposal was that adopted by Mr and Mrs Earl Calhoun of Tulsa. They were in a church service when Mr. Calhoun flicked through the hymnbook and pointed out the words "Every day I need thee more." Mrs Calhoun leafed through a few pages further on and showed him the words, "Take me as I am." He did.

"Eros", the third Greek word for love, refers to mutual attraction between the sexes. This is wonderful and is the heart of romance. In our current society it has often been debased from its true value. True Eros often flourishes as a way of drawing the sexes together and finds its fulfilment in love within marriage. A friend of mine, Ray Mayhew, sends me regular talks on various subjects of interest that he is researching. Recently he stated that in the United States there is an upsurge of interest in the works of Jane Austen. It is as though the young people of America are discovering again that actually there is much to be said for taking the pace of a relationship more slowly and taking time to get to know the other person long before physical intimacy ensues.

This period of romance and growth in relationship is a very important precursor to happy and fulfilled marriage. Jane Austen's books are full of romance but it develops slowly and in stages. There are often hurdles to be overcome before a relationship flowers. Characters are tested until their true nature becomes apparent. This growing together phase is important and cannot be rushed. The sexual aspect of the relationship comes at the end of the process, except for those situations where it is brought forward prematurely as in the case of Lydia in Pride and Prejudice where it all goes wrong. The more we give away of ourselves before marriage the less trusting the marriage is likely to be.

A picture of Eros is given to us in the early chapters of Genesis. Adam and Eve were walking in the garden and were naked and not ashamed. There was mutual attraction, and there was a reciprocal response of love. Those of us who have been to many marriage ceremonies can almost quote the words where it states that marriage is instituted by God to be a source of comfort and companionship. It is for mutual edification and the bringing forth of children. It is to be a blessing to the two people involved; it is to give security to children and stability to society.

The modern western sexual revolution, in attacking marriage, robs people of trust and fulfilment, damages the lives of children and leaves society in tatters. Marriage was God's pattern in the beginning. There is a one-flesh contract within marriage.

In becoming one flesh with another person, much of oneself is given away and much is received in return. This is a solemn contract and can bring great blessing in its train.

A lovely picture of this is given to us in the Song of Solomon. It is a celebration of Eros as given by God to bless mankind. The Bible is not against good wholesome sex. After all God created it! The Song of Solomon is quite sexually explicit, but in a wonderful way. The bride reveals herself only to her lover. There is a commitment to relationship. There is commitment to continuity. The relationship is there to last. Of course many see also, in the Song of Solomon, a picture of the loving attachment between Christ and his church. The bride is the church and Christ is the lover, and the contract is like that of a marriage. We are committed to Christ in love and this commitment takes precedence over all others.

Nuns, in their initiation vows, express this contract by avowing their love for Christ in terms of lasting commitment. Catherine of Siena, a fourteenth century Italian mystic said, "The soul cannot live without loving. It must have something to love, for it was created to love." Mechtilde of Magdeburg, a German nun of the thirteenth century wrote, "Lord, you are my lover, my longing, my flowing stream, my sun, and I am your reflection."

Failure to keep marriage holy and clean has resulted in immense devastation in our current society. Divorce, family breakdown, and rocky, unstable marriages plunge children into a sea of uncertainty about whether they are loved and valued.

They do not know where to turn to find the love that their parents should have provided throughout childhood. The most important thing for a child to experience is a loving bond with its mother, as we have already observed. Probably next in importance is to see father and mother cherishing, respecting and loving each other.

From the bond with its mother the child will know that it is loved and important. From its observation of love in action in the lives of its parents it will carry an understanding of the way relationships are supposed to work. This will help the child in its future relationships with the wider world. Without these key understandings the child is left in a disadvantaged position.

The breakdown of marriage is not something particularly new. Boniface in the eighth century wrote, "If indeed the English people, as is rumoured abroad and cast up against us in France and Italy, despise lawful marriage, a people that is unworthy and degenerate will come into being, and our nation will cease to be strong. We suffer because of the disgraceful conduct of our people." These words, written thirteen centuries ago, still ring true today.

It has been observed that to the extent that a society honours marriage, then it is strong and effective. Societies that place low values on marriage and commitment tend to disintegrate. In Gibbon's The History of the Decline and Fall of the Roman Empire, completed in 1787, several reasons are given for that fall. One of the most important was the rapid increase of divorce which led to the undermining of home life, which is the basis of society.

As one observes the current climate in Great Britain, there are housing estates where drug taking, juvenile alcoholism, crime and violence are rife. This state of affairs is to a large extent related to family breakdown with the decay in our society being caused by the disintegration of its individual components.

Strong family units are built when the other forms of love, which lend it strength and stability, support the Eros of romantic love. When expressed in the context of an ongoing, loving and committed relationship, Eros brings added strength to that relationship. In marriage it will bind together the qualities of Storge or family love, and Philia which is friendship love. Eros will bind and glue the relationship together. Sexual love within marriage is to be enjoyed. It is not only for the procreation of children, which St Augustine would have us believe. Perhaps his wild excesses before his conversion to Christianity led him towards an abstemious position thereafter. Such a viewpoint finds no biblical basis and there is certainly no evidence for it in the Song of Solomon. Sexual love is there to be enjoyed to the full within the marriage relationship.

Sexual love, however, taken outside of the marriage will cause damage to the married couple and to the children of that marriage. When done in secret it will result in hiding and deception which will cloud the relationship and weaken the unit. Besides, on a lighter note, if we believe G K Chesterton, then being married to one woman is rather like being married to a harem. "No doubt, a woman is not today what she will be tomorrow; that is why marriage is so exciting: variability is one of the virtues of woman. It obviates the crude requirements of polygamy. If you have one good wife, you are sure to have a spiritual harem." "Domestic life is full of surprises; mere love affairs are apt to be monotonous." Or again "One sun is splendid, six suns would be only vulgar ... The poetry of love is in following the single woman ... the poetry of religion in worshipping the single star."

The observation of Chesterton is that one woman is never the same. She changes in time. She changes during the week. Certainly from close observation of my wife I can confirm his statement! Every marriage changes over time. At times it may seem that Eros is weak, at other times it will be very strong. The marriage may go through stormier times, as difficult decisions need to be made, or there are struggles and pain with children. Eros certainly helps to hold it together, though is insufficient by itself to withstand the pressures. A resilient and strong marriage will also have the love of friendship, the Storge of committed family relationships and will be undergirded with the last of these facets of love which is Agape love.

What's In A Sacrifice?

There was a certain emperor Shah Abbas who ruled in great style in Persia. He quite enjoyed mixing with the people when disguised and, dressed as a poor man, he used to go down a long flight of stairs to a tiny cellar where a fire attendant seated on the ash heap used to look after the fires. He would sit down beside him and begin to talk about all kinds of matters, and ask the man for his opinions. When it was lunchtime the fire attendant brought out coarse, black bread and a jug of water and they ate and drank together. The Shah went away but kept coming back for his heart was outgoing towards the lonely man. He sometimes gave his advice and the two became good friends. As time went on the emperor thought "I will tell him who I really am and see what gift he would like me to give." On telling the man that he was really the emperor he expected a request for some great favour or reward. The man sat silent however and said,

"Yes, my lord, I understand. But why did you leave your palace in glory to sit with me in this dark place, to eat my poor food and to take an interest in whether I am happy or sad? Even you can give nothing more precious. You may give others rich presents but to me you have given yourself. I would only like to ask you never to withdraw your friendship."

The emperor was willing to stoop down and meet the poor fire attendant in his humble station. Although he came from a highly exalted position, he did not hesitate to take an interest in and care for this lonely man as he tended the fire. Christ shows this kind of love but to a much greater extent. In Philippians 2:6-8 we read these words about Jesus Christ. "Although he existed in the form of God ... [he] emptied himself, taking the form of a bondservant, and being made in the likeness of men. Being found in appearance as a man, he humbled himself by becoming obedient to the point of death, even death on a cross."

Christ himself came down and made much more of a descent than Shah Abbas. The Almighty, only begotten Son, the living Word humbled himself to become a seed in the womb of a virgin. He lived day by day a humble life of sacrifice. He spent himself meeting the needs of the poor, the sick, the hungry and the dying. He then became "obedient even to death on a cross."

This kind of love stoops down to pick up the pieces of a lost and broken humanity. As it stoops, it enters death itself and conquers death. Not only that but, through death and resurrection, lifts up that broken humanity and gives each individual tremendous significance and value. As the fire attendant felt so valued as a result of the friendship of the Shah, so we become highly valued and precious as we relate to the living Christ. This sacrificial love is given the Greek word "Agape."

Agape was a word used rarely in the time of Christ. However as the Greek and Roman world stood astonished at the life of sacrifice shown by the early Christian, they used the word Agape to describe this new phenomenon. It was a love that would do anything for another person. It was a love that would serve and lay down its life not only for its friends but also for its enemies. It was a love that was unafraid to go to death for the love of Christ. It penetrated deep into the soul as individuals realized the extent of the love of Christ for them. In response, the early Christian thought it not too great a sacrifice to pour him or herself out for the world. The Roman world stood back in amazement as it witnessed such transformed lives.

Mel Gibson's film The Passion of The Christ had unprecedented worldwide appeal. Even throughout the Arab world it has met with rapturous audiences. It tells of the passion and suffering of Christ in the days leading up to the crucifixion although not everyone who sees the film will realize that the purpose of the passion and suffering was for him or herself personally.

Throughout his ministry, Jesus was moved with compassion for the crowds and the individuals hidden in the crowds that he alone could perceive. Who else would have picked out a Zacchaeus up a tree, or stopped to heal a crooked and bent old woman? His eyes penetrated the exterior to look on the heart. This compassion, and the power of his miracles brought envy and hostility from the religious leadership. Their hatred was used by God to lead to the path that Christ had already chosen for himself, which inexorably led on to the passion that the film portrays. Compassion led to the passion. Archbishop Temple wrote, "Love of God is the root. Love of our neighbour the fruit of the tree of life. Neither can exist without the other, but the one is cause and the other effect."

As this Agape love transforms our lives then the fruit of that love is love for our neighbour and love for our enemy. As G K Chesterton wrote, "The Bible tells us to love our neighbours and also to love our enemies; probably because they are generally the same people!" When the love of Christ enters into our hearts it brings transformation in our lives. We are set ablaze with love. John Wesley was asked to what he owed his success. He replied, "I set myself on fire, and others come to watch me burn." Agape love penetrates our hearts and sets us ablaze.

The story of the conversion of John Wesley has an interesting background with its roots being traced back in part to a German, Count Zinzendorf. He was very rich, having inherited large lands and estates in his late teenage years. From an early age he had committed himself to loving and following Christ. While still a teenager he was touring Europe and visited an art gallery where he saw a picture by Domenico Feti of the suffering Christ. Underneath the picture were the words "All this I gave for you, what have you given for me?" As Zinzendorf gazed at this picture, his heart was moved within him. He came back the next day, and the next after that, and gazed at this picture. Finally he broke down and recommitted everything in his life to following Christ.

Faced with the amazing love of Christ his life was transformed. He opened up his estates at Herrnhut for persecuted believers. They flocked there in their hundreds. They came from many different religious traditions and sadly brought their divisions with them, leading to major confrontation between the different religious groupings. Zinzendorf, in the midst of the strife, became a peacemaker and after some time there began to be a hunger for the presence of God. One day there was a mighty outpouring of the Holy Spirit upon them as they gathered together. At this meeting the Holy Spirit came down in power and from being separate and disunited the community came together in love and unity. From this one meeting a prayer meeting started which continued 24 hours a day, seven days a week for 100 years!

From that group at Herrnhut (literally "the Lord's Watch") missionaries moved out to many different parts of the world. Some of these Moravian missionaries met John Wesley as he was returning from America, disillusioned with his lack of success. Wesley was in spiritual turmoil. He could not easily believe and could find no assurance in his heart of forgiveness and peace. He was considering giving up as a minister. They wisely counselled him not to give up despite his internal struggles. They said, "Preach faith until you have it, and then preach faith because you have it!"

John Wesley was encouraged and inspired by these Moravian brethren. The love that had burned into Zinzendorf now began to burn in his own heart. He went back to England, met Christ in a new way, and his life was full of the power of God. He travelled many thousands of miles by horseback all over the British Isles. The brothers John and Charles Wesley, in the space of a generation, transformed the spiritual climate of England. It began when Zinzendorf saw the picture of the suffering Christ. The love of Christ penetrated his heart and transformed him. It has always been this way. Agape love by its very nature is transforming.

It is this kind of love that we seek to have in our hearts. If this love is in our hearts then God will help us overcome our failures and difficulties and he will work through us. God's love comes into the core of our being. As our spirits are inspired and moved by the love of God, so that fire of love begins to move out through our bodies and our souls to bring life into the world.

God will bring us the opportunities to express this love. Friends of mine recently invited me to Bulgaria to visit an orphanage. Because of generous donations received from many different people, we were able to take 50 orphans away for a week. This was the first time that many of these orphans had ever been on holiday. Despite being with them for only this short time, at the end of our time it was extremely difficult to leave. Most of the team, including myself, were in tears as we left. I can vividly picture a five-year-old boy, dressed in dirty shorts, tee shirt and a pair of trainers.

As we were leaving he said to a member of the team, "I never learned to love until you came along." Hearing that caused my heart to melt with a whole mixture of emotions. There was the pain and sadness of leaving. There was the overwhelming sense of unmet need in the hearts of the orphans. But at the same time there was a deep sense of thankfulness that God had helped us as a team to show these orphans something of his love. If we can love in such a way that others too will learn to love, everything becomes worthwhile.

God is supremely the God of the poor and destitute. He loves the alien, the orphan and the widow and those who feel forsaken by all, even God himself. This feeling was experienced by Jesus who knew what it felt like to be forsaken of the Father for a time, whilst hanging on the cross, so he could clasp the world to his heart. Jesus plumbed the depths of this experience so that he might identify with those who feel themselves to be forsaken by God himself. On the cross, Jesus felt separated from God the Father for a time as he bore the sin of the world. Through this outstanding act of love he has made himself fully available to those who by their circumstances seem to be godforsaken. Graham Kendrick wrote these words expressing this love on the heart of God.

> God of the poor, friend of the weak,
> Give us compassion we pray.
> Melt our cold hearts,
> Let tears flow like rain,
> Come change our love,
> From a spark to a flame.

At Christmas time we particularly associate the coming of Christ into the world with the desire to help those less fortunate than ourselves. I like what G K Chesterton wrote regarding this: "Anyone thinking of the holy child as born in December would mean by it exactly what we mean by it; that Christ is not merely a summer sun of the prosperous but a winter fire for the unfortunate." The heart of God reaches out to the lost and dying of the world. We owe it to the love of God that we have experienced, to seek with Agape love those for whom God's heart bleeds.

William Booth wrote, "Every cab-horse in London is given food, shelter and work. People ought to be looked after just as well as a cab-horse is cared for." He recognized the needs of the destitute and the dying and did something about it. The work of the Salvation Army brought transformation to many, many lives, first in East London and then throughout the world. He went on to say, "While women weep, as they do now, I'll fight; or men go to prison in and out, in and out, as they do now, I'll fight. While there is a drunkard left, while there is a lost girl on the streets, where there remains one dark soul without the light of God, I'll fight! I'll fight to the very end!"

The difficulty today is that most people seek to exclude or ridicule the love of Christ. Thomas Carlyle, the Scottish historian, wrote, "If Jesus Christ would come today people would not even crucify him. They would ask him to dinner, and hear what he has to say, and make fun of it." The tragedy is that this Agape love is often ignored or ridiculed, rather than being lived and sadly many find the sacrifice too costly in their own lives.

CHAPTER 4

GOD'S PHOTOGRAPH

—⁓—

What Love Creates

Some time ago there was a most unusual radio broadcast in Puerto Rico as a result of which couples were rushing to the altar as fast as they possibly could. In early June there had been a radio broadcast to say that all Caza would be prohibited. Now Caza sounds like Casar. These words may seem very similar, but they mean quite different things in Puerto Rico. Caza means hunting whilst Casar means marriage. Some Puerto Ricans, as a result of the broadcast, believed that by 10 June of that year all weddings would be prohibited and you could no longer get married in Puerto Rico. That was why so many couples were rushing to the altar while there was still time. You can imagine the feelings of those who found that they had jumped rather hastily into matrimony just because of that radio broadcast.

By contrast God loves to communicate clearly. The Holy Trinity at some stage in the distant past decided to share the love and harmony they enjoyed by making man in their own image. Man could then share in love with his creator. He could come into the divine fellowship that had existed for all eternity and share in the heart of God. In making man a free agent, God was already committing himself to the process of redemption by paying an infinite price, the death of his dearly beloved Son. The Son is described as being slain from the creation, or foundation of the world. (Revelation 13:8) Christ had decided even before the world was created that he would come and suffer to redeem mankind. The love in the heart of God seeks to embrace the whole of humanity. The Trinity in unison created mankind. The Trinity would also bring about its redemption.

Creation is the communication of the love on the heart of God. God is love, and he wants others to share in that love. Love exists in relationships. Love is the heartbeat of the Trinity. God desires others to share this wonderful experience of self-giving, genuine love. He does this through the creation of other beings who share his very image and likeness. (Genesis 1:26)

This same desire to create is true of family life. The husband and wife love to create. There is risk involved. One never quite knows how the offspring will turn out. The risk seems worth taking. The desire to share love with sons and daughters is a very strong driving force. (Not that all children are necessarily conceived with quite these thoughts in mind!) It is a tremendous joy when children are born. The pain and sorrow of labour is forgotten with the wonderful cry of the newborn infant.

If human love loves to create, the same is true of divine love. Love by its nature wants to expand and fill the universe with itself. It longs to build unity and togetherness between people, and between people and God himself. It reaches out to bring others into loving relationship. Love is the prime mover behind the universe. God moves in response to love. That love creates and it heals. It expands and brings blessing and is there to fill the world with itself.

A few years ago I decided that it would be a good idea to breed thoroughbred rabbits. I thought this would be a useful income and I could train the children in the ways of business and making money. They would clean the cages out and feed the rabbits. I would take the young rabbits to the shops to sell them and then plough the money back into the business. In this way I would demonstrate to the children how money could be made. It was to be a small-business operation. Of course the inevitable happened. And guess who cleaned the hutches! Guess who fed the rabbits! However the girls were delighted to find the furry balls of baby rabbits nestling in the corner of the hutch.

One unforgettable hot summer's day I was driving to the pet shop to sell the rabbits. The car suddenly chugged to a halt on a motorway slipway in a most unfortunate and perilous position. Not only did I have a number of baby rabbits on board but also several lively children bouncing up and down in the back seat. My wife had to rescue the children and the rabbits before the car was finally towed away and so we survived! I am relieved that I no longer breed pet rabbits.

There is a joy in observing nature take its course to bring about reproduction and multiplication. This is not to suggest however that we should breed quite as freely as the rabbits! Laws of reproduction in nature reflect the heart of God who loves to create. Love starts the whole process.

Nature expresses the heart of God. William Cowper said, "Nature is but a name for an effect whose cause is God." God is a God who loves to create and to make things new. Gerard Manley Hopkins, an English poet wrote,

> The world is charged with the grandeur of
> God,
> It will flame out, like shining from shook
> foil;
> It gathers to greatness, like the ooze of oil
> crushed.
> Why do men then now not reck his rod?

There is grandeur in the creation that stems from the God who loves to create and fill the world with love and beauty. Francis Bacon, an English philosopher and essayist, stated "I'd rather believe all the fables in the legends in the Talmud and the Al-Coran than that this universal frame is without a mind." George Macdonald said, "God's fingers can touch nothing but to mould it into loveliness."

God's heart of love is seen in the creation of man in his image and is seen in the natural world in the laws of reproduction and fruitfulness. (Genesis 1:20-31) God is the initiator and sustainer of life. There has never been a satisfactory answer to how the universe could arise by itself without there being a prime mover and creator behind the process. When considering the origin of things, it is not just the physical world that needs explanation, it is also the spiritual. Without God, how did love itself originate? Where is the origin of a love that will move a Mother Teresa or a Damien or a Booth, unless it is from God himself? There seems to be no rational or evolutionary argument that can satisfactorily explain altruistic love and sacrifice.

In this section we have considered the desire that there is in God to create and make others like himself. This likeness reflects the nature of the creator who is perfect love. Yet at the same time, this image has been fashioned in amazing ways to create immense variety amongst those who bear his image. In the human race there is the celebration of unity in being made in the likeness of the creator. At the same time there is the celebration of diversity as we observe the many different ways in which that image is displayed. God in love desired to fill the world with his image and likeness, so that love would pervade the whole universe with its fragrant aroma. This would result in a universe filled with peace, harmony and order. Let us look more closely now at this image that God has created.

Man, The Photograph Of God

Leonardo da Vinci was searching for someone to sit as a model for Christ in his painting of the Last Supper. He found a young man called Pietro Bandinelli who sang in the choir in one of the churches of Rome. Years later the picture was nearing completion. He had painted every disciple except Judas Iscariot. Now he tried to find a man whose face was hard and distorted by sin. In the end, he found a beggar on the streets of Rome with a face so villainous that he trembled when he looked at him. He asked the man to sit for him as he began to paint the face of Judas in the picture. When he was about to send the man on his way he said, "I don't yet know your name." The man retorted that the famous artist was already acquainted with him. "I am Pietro Bandinelli", he stated, "I also sat for you as a model of Christ."

God has chosen that we should bear his family likeness. The image which we share is the image of God himself. The likeness of God has been planted in man. This image may become so marred as to be almost unrecognizable. Our appearance may change according to what we do with our lives. One of the beauties of the Christian faith is that as we continue to look at Christ we become more like him. The Bible talks about us being changed into his likeness. (2 Corinthians 3:18) "But we all with unveiled face, beholding as in a mirror the glory of the Lord, are being transformed into the same image from glory to glory, just as from the Lord, the Spirit."

As we look at Christ, we take on more and more the likeness of God himself. So the image of God within all of us, because all mankind is made in his image, can either become more and more like God himself or it can be progressively destroyed. Although we may not have the gifts of Handel or Leonardo da Vinci, we can each use the gifts given to us by God to reflect his glory in this world.

Someone who has used the gifts God has given her in outstanding ways is Baroness Caroline Cox. She could have remained in her position and worked hard as a nurse. She knew, on the other hand, that she could not ignore the tremendous needs in the Sudan. Her visits to this war-ravaged country, including dangerous forbidden areas, have numbered at least twenty-seven. She has walked through land-mined areas in Burma and Nagorno Karabakh. In Russia she helped transform childcare for orphans from large impersonal state-run orphanages, which by their nature were unable to give children the love and care they need, to family foster care. During the Cold War she delivered medical aid to Poland. She has been a bold advocate for the poor. As a deputy speaker in the House of Lords she has spoken for those who cannot speak up for themselves.

She describes herself as "a nurse and social scientist by intention and a politician by astonishment." Yet she also admits to a "fit of faithless, fearful dread" before going on her more dangerous missions. Before going to Nagorno Karabakh at the height of the conflict between Armenia and Azerbaijan she remembers "feeling dark and not wanting to go."

Baroness Cox counts it a privilege to risk her life to help others, although she is in many ways just an ordinary person, like you and me, who has allowed herself to be used by God. Despite tremendous fear and opposition she has kept going to reach out to the world in love. In the same way, God can take each of our lives with the gifts that he has given us, and use them for his glory.

Let us look in more detail now and consider what it means to bear the image of God. What does this word "image" really mean? The word that is mainly used expresses a very close likeness or similarity. Christ is called the image of God. Colossians 1:15 states, "He is the image of the invisible God." The word used is "Icon". An icon is a representation. It was used in Greek to mean a portrait. It is the nearest Greek word to our word "photograph". It was also used as a way of ratifying a contract where the icon was a brief summary of the personal characteristics or distinguishing marks of the contracting parties.

When we transfer these concepts to what the Bible is saying when it talks about Jesus Christ as the Icon of God, it is in effect saying that Jesus is the picture, or the photograph or the summary of God himself. And when it states that we are made in the image of God similar meanings are conveyed. In Genesis 1:27 we read "God created man in his own image, in the image of God he created him; male and female he created them."

As Christ demonstrated to the world the image of God, so man also shows the image of God. Psalm 8 talks about man and his relationship to God in these terms. Verses 5-8 say, "Yet you have made him a little lower than God and you crown him with glory and majesty! You make him to rule over the work of your hands, you have put all things under his feet, all sheep and oxen and also the beasts of the field, the birds of the heavens and the fish of the sea, whatever passes through the paths of the seas." It is a wonderful privilege to be made in the image of God.

In what way is this image expressed? Many people throughout Christian history have sought to explain the meaning of the image of God in us. St Thomas Aquinas stated that the image of God in human form is expressed in human ability to think and reason, to use language and art surpassing the ability of the animals. Leonard Verduin, a contemporary pastor and author, stated that the image was encapsulated in our dominion over animals and plants which continues despite our sinfulness. Francis Schaeffer, a North American theologian, has said, "Man, made in the image of God, has a purpose – to be in relationship to God who is there. Man forgets his purpose and thus he forgets who he is and what life means. Made in God's image, man was made to be great. He was made to be beautiful and he was made to be creative in life and art. But his rebellion has led him into making himself into nothing but a machine."

Dorothy Sayers, an English writer of detective stories and Christian apologist, has said, "Work is the natural exercise and function of man, the creature who is made in the image of his creator." Evdokimov, a Russian Orthodox lay theologian, has stated, "Man is free for he is the image of divine liberty: and that is why he has the power to choose." Dorothy Day, a North American Catholic writer and social reformer, has said, "God is our creator. God made us in his image and likeness. Therefore we are creators. The joy of creativeness should be ours. God gave us a garden to till and cultivate. We became co-creators by our responsible acts, whether in bringing forth children or producing food, furniture or clothing."

These sayings emphasize different aspects of what it means to be made in the image of God. There is the joy of creativity which is often beautifully expressed in art and music. Handel's Messiah was written within three weeks – a prodigious feat. Handel penned it with tears in his eyes especially when he came to the part, "He was despised and rejected." He could not write without the sacrifice of Christ touching the depths of his being.

It is amazing to consider that some of the greatest musicians composed their finest, most memorable works in the face of almost impossible physical handicaps. Beethoven's Ninth Symphony including "Ode to Joy" must surely be one of the most outstanding pieces of music the world has known. However Beethoven himself could not hear it being performed owing to late-onset deafness. His "Moonlight Sonata" was written to enable a blind girl to sense in some way what it meant to be under the spell of the still and silvery light of the moon.

As God himself loves to create so he has passed on to man, his image, this same desire to create. This is seen in many different realms of human endeavour. The glory of man is seen in the beauty he creates in such giftings as art and music. His tragedy is when that creativity is warped and corrupted through external pressure, whether that is political, religious or the result of the struggle just to survive.

Art demonstrates man's creative energy. Michelangelo skilfully fashioned a most beautiful statue of Moses. On completion of this sculpture he went up to the statue, which was so lifelike, and attacked it with a chisel saying, "Why then, dost thou not speak?" The arts and music and all life and human endeavour express the creativity planted within us by God.

Work is another expression of the image of God in us. The picture given to us in Genesis 2:2 is of God resting after completing his work. "By the seventh day God completed his work which he had done, and he rested on the seventh day from all his work which he had done." Cycles of work and rest seem to be normative for us. This cycle most naturally follows a seven-day period. Attempts to change this cycle, as happened during the French Revolution, have tended to be short lived.

As God worked and enjoyed it, so his intention is that man, his image, should also enjoy work and find it fulfilling. When God placed Adam and Eve in a beautiful garden, he taught them to look after it and he also taught them to name the animals. This picture shows us that man was made to be responsible for the animal kingdom and for the plant kingdom; and to treat them with care and attention. The world may be seen as a love gift from God, our creator to each one of us. We can enjoy it and be blessed by it but we must treat it responsibly. We can be fulfilled in looking after and caring for it. We can be responsible in animal husbandry, agriculture and in caring for world resources. There are unending opportunities for creative work in the world. If this work is unavailable in certain parts of the world, then we have a corporate duty to help these people find work opportunities. We cannot sit back and allow the developing world to endure massive unemployment or horrendous toil with very limited returns. Inequity of employment opportunities and unfair trade agreements need concerted action by those of us in more privileged situations.

Looking after the physical world is important. An old man was asked about his beautiful garden. He talked at great length about what he had done in the garden. His inquisitor was dismissive. "Well, it was God who helped you do it." The man wisely replied, "You should have seen the garden when God had it to himself!" God has given us the raw materials. It is up to us to use these raw materials and through our work to express the creativity that God has planted within us. God has called us to be wise stewards of the world. The world is his love gift to us to be thoroughly enjoyed but we need to treat it responsibly.

Creativity and work are part of being made in the image of God. God is himself continuing to work. He is not absent. He is not somehow winding the world up and leaving it to run by itself. Rather he is intimately involved with us in relationship. He is working his purposes out and expects us to work with him.

Multiplication is also on the heart of God. He blessed Adam and Eve in the garden, saying "Be fruitful and multiply." Fruitfulness is not only procreation and population growth; it is the spreading out of the image of God into the world. It was the way to bring the whole world into order, the order of God. Reproduction, multiplication, and filling the world with love are part of his intention.

One of the beauties of being made in the image of God is that it makes man to be great and important. Psalm 8:5 reads, "Yet you have made him for a little while lower than God, and you crown him with glory and majesty!" We are very special. We are made a little lower than God himself. All of us are extremely important. Realizing this gives us great self-worth and value. Moore has said, "A sense of human greatness is the threshold of belief." We are made in his very image.

Thomas Aquinas stated that reason was part of the creative image. This is important. Our logic and reason are part of the image that God has placed within us. Our abilities to reason and to use judgment are part of our creative image.

As we are made in the image of God, then part of the expression of this image will be seen in the way that we relate to our creator. God intended this. The creator wants to enjoy a close relationship with the created through worship. There is a tendency in all people groups to have different forms of worship. Worldwide there is that pervasive sense that we are not alone in the universe. There is a reaching out from our hearts to something that is beyond us. This is expressed in all societies and in all forms of worship. There is something internal to us that is reaching out and saying, "I am more than a collection of atoms." As Jonathan Swift said, "That the universe was formed by a fortuitous concourse of atoms, I will no more believe than that the accidental jumbling of the alphabet would fall into a most ingenious treatise of Philosophy."

Indeed as William Shakespeare has said "What a piece of work is man! How noble in reason! How infinite in faculty! In form, in moving how express and admirable, in action how like an angel, in apprehension how like a god! The beauty of the world! The paragon of animals!" (Hamlet 2 ii, 115-117) All of these emphasize the importance and the greatness of man. That greatness is seen primarily as man is in relationship with God himself. It is as man enjoys that relationship with his creator that he grows into the fullness of his image. Irenaeus said, "God made man lord of the earth, but he was small, being but a child. He had to grow and reach full maturity." As we mature in this relationship with God, so we are able to show this world the very nature of God.

When God created man in his own image he created them "male and female." The masculine and feminine, the male and female express the image of God. The commands in Genesis 1:28 "Be fruitful and multiply and fill the earth and subdue it; and rule over the fish of the sea and over the birds of the sky and over every living thing that moves on the earth," were given to man and woman together. God further emphasized this truth by taking woman from a rib in man's side. As someone has wisely said, "Eve was taken out of the side of Adam; not from his head so that he could rule over her, and not from his feet so that he could tread on her, but from his side so that she could be with him, and support and comfort him, and bring him companionship." Man and woman being together, and working side by side in common purpose, reflect his glory. As man and woman work and relate together in harmony and unity, the fullness of the image of God will be seen.

Why should this be so? Relationships of love on earth reflect the heavenly relationships of love. These are between God the Father, God the Son and God the Holy Spirit. In family life as man, woman and child flow together in harmony and love, the image of God may be seen. In the New Testament, the image of God is seen not so much in individuals, but rather as people relate together in the new community. This community is called his body which is creative in its essence. It lives and moves to show God to the world. The church is the body of Christ. Only as it works together in harmony and loving relationship can it show Christ to the world. No man can do this fully by himself as no man is an island. We can only do this as we live together in love and unity. The community then expresses God's purposes, and God's will and presence are made known to the world.

Christ, The Perfect Photograph

This is the story of Rabbi Joshua in the time of the Roman Emperor, Trajan. He had a rather gruesome appearance. The children used to mock him in the street. The Emperor's daughter approached him one day and said to him with a smile, "How is it that such great wisdom as yours should be contained in an ugly head?" He responded, "In what vessels does the Emperor, your father, keep his wine?" "In earthen jars," she replied. "Really!" exclaimed the rabbi, "All the common people keep wine in earthen jars. The Emperor should keep his in better vessels."

Thinking he really meant what he said, the princess had the butler pour all the wine into gold and silver vessels. Of course when it was poured out it was totally sour as the metal reacted with the wine. When the girl met the rabbi again she upbraided him for his seemingly bad advice. He said wisely, "You have learned, princess, a simple lesson. Wine is best kept in common vessels: so is wisdom." Christ has similarly chosen that his best wine be kept in simple vessels. As Paul states "But God has chosen the foolish things of the world to shame the wise, and God has chosen the weak things of the world to shame the things which are strong ... so that no man may boast before God." (1 Corinthians 1:27-29)

In our weakness we are called to show God's image to the world. That image will be seen as we take seriously the needs of the poor and those who cannot speak up for themselves, as Baroness Cox has done. God is calling us to show the world his nature at work within us. He is calling us to pour ourselves out for the poor and needy and to care for his world. Practically this involves conservation as well as the care and cure of the individual. It means being a friend of the earth as well as a friend of the poor. It means cutting down on the use of non-renewable energy sources. It affects our daily decisions and our driving habits. We want to leave this world to future posterity in at least as good a state as we found it! Living out the image of God in the world affects all aspects of our behaviour. In all of this we will not succeed in living up perfectly to the image Christ has put within us. But we can do our best with his help.

One of the chief objectives of Christ as he prepared to leave his disciples was for them to share his joy. Parents delight to give joy to their children. So Jesus wants us to share in the joy that he has in his relationship with the Father. That may seem impossible in a world of pain. The truth however is that no one faced more suffering and pain than Christ himself. Joy is a mindset of thankfulness to God in every situation. Jesus says, "But now I come to you; and these things I speak in the world so that they may have my joy made full in themselves." (John 17:13) St Thomas Aquinas says, "Happiness is the natural life of man." He continues, "Sheer joy is God's, and this demands companionship." As we relate to God as Father, and as we experience the presence of Christ in our lives, then we become to the world the reflection of God's very nature. We are called to reflect the glory of God. This is a wonderful calling and should fill us with anticipation and joy as we face each day.

One of the beauties about being created in the image of God is that we are in a unique position between God and the created world. Indeed it is through man that the created world can respond and relate to God. For example, the animals were brought to Adam for him to name. In the age to come it is promised that the lion will lie down with the lamb. Man is now given the responsibility for looking after creation, so creation itself can be united to God through man. God is interested in reconciliation for all things. He wishes now to delegate his rule in the world he created to man. Before, this seemed an impossible task to a wounded and damaged image. Now with the image remade, who knows what may be possible? Certainly there are stories of men who seem to have a strange power over the animal kingdom. St Francis of Assisi had this ability. Sadhu Sundar Singh of India is a more recent example.

As we open our hearts to receive more of God's Spirit, so we become more and more like Christ. We share more of his very nature and as Paul says, "We ... are being transformed into the same image, from glory to glory."(2 Corinthians 3:18.) This gives man, in relationship with God, a unique position in the world. In this bond God entrusts him with similar instructions as Adam received. These are to look after the world, to care for the animal kingdom and to demonstrate to the world the presence of God. We may feel weak and inadequate for the task. Yet in our weakness we are called upon to carry the goods of heaven in our hearts. "What can I do for God today?" might be the question in my heart. "What new thing can I create in God's name?" The image portrayed by man is of course imperfect. Rather than having a perfect photograph, the image is blurred and indistinct. In Christ however we can see the perfect image.

It is interesting to note that even Napoleon Bonaparte could recognize the uniqueness of Christ.

"I know men; and I tell you that Jesus Christ is not a man. Superficial minds see a resemblance between Christ and the founders of empires, and the gods of other religions. That resemblance does not exist. There is between Christianity and whatever other religions the distance of infinity ... Everything in Christ astonishes me. His spirit overawes me and his will confounds me. Between him and whoever else in the world, there is no possible term of comparison. He is truly a being by himself. His ideas and sentiments and the truth he announces, his manner of convincing are not explained either by human organization or by the nature of things ... The nearer I approach, the more carefully I examine, everything is above me, everything remains grand, of a grandeur which overpowers. His religion is a revelation from an intelligence which certainly is not of man ... One can absolutely find nowhere but in him alone the imitation or the example of his life ... I search in vain in history to find the similar to Jesus Christ, or anything which can approach the gospel. Neither history nor humanity, nor the ages, nor nature, offer me anything with which I am able to compare it or explain it. Here everything is extraordinary."(Henry Parry Lidden, Lidden's Bamford Lectures)

Napoleon certainly recognized the supremacy of Christ. Many in this world whilst applauding the teachings of Christ appear content to leave him outside of their lives. Whilst he can be relegated to the position of a good moral teacher, then there is little necessity to treat his claims seriously and he can be ignored. Such is the popular myth in our current post-Christian society in Britain. However this position does not stand up to careful analysis.

C S Lewis was keen to point out that many of the things that people say about Christ are completely illogical. For example, some have stated that Christ is a great moral teacher but no more than that. These people tend to declare confidently that he is not the Son of God. Lewis points out the inherent illogicality of such statements. If a mere man made the claims that Jesus did, for example "I am the bread of life" (John 6:35) and "I am the light of the world" (John 8:12) then he would not be a great moral teacher. He would be either badly deluded needing medical help, or he would be amongst the worst deceivers known to mankind, or he would be whom he confessed himself to be, the Son of the Father – God himself. (See John 5:19 for one place where Jesus claims this unique relationship.)

By no analysis could he be simply a great moral teacher. C S Lewis explains, "You can shut him up for a fool, you can spit at him and kill him as a demon; or you can fall at his feet and call him Lord and God, but let us not come up with any patronizing nonsense about his being a great human teacher. He has not left that open to us. He did not intend to." When we look at Christ we observe his supreme teachings, we gaze with admiration and awe on his miraculous works that flow from his heart of compassion, we admire intensely his courage and integrity and we bow in worship in the face of his willingness to pay the ultimate sacrifice.

Jesus says regarding this laying down of his life. "For this reason the Father loves me because I lay down my life so that I may take it again. No-one has taken it from me but I lay it down on my own initiative, I have authority to lay it down and I have authority to take it up again." (John 10:17-18) Not only was Christ totally different from all others, but he also had the power over his own life both to lay it down and then to take it up again. This is the life that has had such an impact down through the ages.

The famous essay "One Solitary Life" illustrates the impact made by this one life.

"Here is a man who was born in an obscure village, the child of a peasant woman. He grew up in another village. He worked in a carpenter's shop until he was 30, and then for three years he was an itinerant preacher. He never owned a home. He never wrote a book. He never held an office. He never had a family. He never went to college. He never put his foot inside a big city. He never travelled 200 miles from the place he was born. He never did one of the things that usually accompany greatness. He had no credentials but himself ... While still a young man the tide of popular opinion turned against him. His friends ran away. One of them denied him. He was turned over to his enemies. He went through the mockery of a trial. He was nailed on a cross between two thieves. Whilst he was dying his executioners gambled for the only piece of property he had on earth, his coat. When he was dead he was taken down and laid in a borrowed grave, through the pity of a friend.

"Nineteen full centuries have come and gone, and today he is the centrepiece of the human race and the leader of the column of progress. I am far within the mark, when I say that all the armies that ever marched, all the navies that were ever built, all the parliaments that ever sat and all the kings that ever reigned, put together have not affected the life of man upon this earth as powerfully as has that one solitary life." (Anonymous)

Christ is unique amongst men. Yet he imparts to us his Spirit so we may be like him. John 20:22 says, "And when he had said this he breathed on them and said to them, 'Receive the Holy Spirit.'" Christ, who is so different from all others who have ever lived, loves us so much that he gives us of his Spirit so we can be like him. The image of God that we all share through being creatures of God has become warped and damaged, but Christ makes it new. As it says "Therefore if anyone is in Christ, he is a new creature."(2 Corinthians 5:17)

God's Photograph And Man's Reason

Sir Isaac Newton had a perfect replica of our solar system made in miniature. In the centre was the sun with all the planets revolving around it. A scientist, who was also an atheist, entered Newton's study one day and exclaimed, "My! What an exquisite thing this is! Who made it?" "Nobody!" replied Newton, to which the scientist replied, "You must think I'm a fool! Of course somebody made it, and he is a genius." Then Isaac Newton put a hand on his friend's shoulder and said, "This thing is but a puny imitation of a much grander system whose laws you and I know. And I am not able to convince you that this mere toy is without a designer and maker, yet you profess to believe that the great original from which this design is taken has come into being without designer or maker. But tell me, by what sort of reasoning do you reach such incongruous conclusions?"

Einstein said, "I want to know his thoughts, the rest are details." He also said, "God does not play dice with the universe." Newton and Einstein, probably accepted by virtually everyone as the two outstanding figures in scientific progress, believed in a God who planned the universe. They were simply thinking God's thoughts after him.

St Thomas Aquinas made this statement, "Reason in man is rather like God in the world." What he is saying is that our abilities to reason and think logically are expressions of God's image in our lives.

There are some verses in the Bible that are commonly misunderstood because they are read out of context. Read in isolation, they at first sight seem to excuse our inability to understand God's ways. This is the position taken by many Christians today. Faced with something that is apparently illogical, instead of trying to grapple with the problem, they will assert,

"God's ways are not our ways." In so doing, they opt out of the difficulty rather than seeking to explore the area of conflict more thoroughly, with the hope of reaching a satisfactory conclusion. These are the verses in their context. Isaiah 55:6-9: "Seek the Lord while he may be found; Call upon him while he is near; let the wicked forsake his way, and the unrighteous man his thoughts; And let him return to the Lord, and he will have compassion on him, and to our God for he will abundantly pardon." And then come these words, "'For my thoughts are not your thoughts nor are your ways my ways,' declares the Lord. 'For as the heavens are higher than the earth, so are my ways higher than your ways and my thoughts than your thoughts.'"

God is not saying here that his thoughts are unintelligible. Rather he is contrasting the ways of wickedness and the ways of goodness. He is contrasting the ways of God as shown in life and mercy from the ways of wickedness and unrighteousness, which were the ways of his people. He is inviting us to seek him and turn from our wicked ways because our thoughts are not his thoughts. In other words, the ways of his people were wicked and their thoughts were wicked. He is not saying in these verses that he cannot be understood.

The Christian Church has commonly misunderstood this. It has automatically taken these verses to mean that we cannot possibly understand God's ways and God's ways are past finding out. If we are given logic and reason as part of the image of God inside us, then that logic and reason have the ability to think out and to discern God's ways. We are using God's image (in logic and reason) to discern God's ways.

This means that if we come to a conclusion that can be shown to be logical, then that conclusion is probably right. There may be mistakes in our logic that another will point out. But the rules of logic seem to be built into our make-up and are the foundation of the sciences and medicine. In these disciplines, those who have instructed us have taken care in their teaching to point out our errors of logic, so that we do not make the same mistakes again.

In the area of theology it would seem that a different principle seems to operate in the minds of some people. If a conclusion is reached that is logical but does not seem to fit with an equally good but separate logical conclusion, we adopt a different strategy rather than seeking to harmonize the two conclusions as would be done in the sciences. We say that the two will not harmonize. For example we may state, on the one hand, that God foreordains each individual for either hell or heaven prior to birth. We will also state, on the other hand, that each individual can make a totally free choice to come to God. On simply logical grounds these two statements are irreconcilable. In this type of dilemma many will use the above verses to dodge the obvious illogicality. Many will say something like this; "Because God's thoughts are higher than our thoughts, then he knows the answer to this dilemma, and we do not need to concern ourselves about the issues further." One would never get away with this in the sciences! (For further reading on this particular point I recommend

God's Strategy in Human History by Forster and Marston, which deals with the issues in depth.)

If we come to the conclusion that something is illogical, then to put God in front of the problem does not solve the illogicality. Even if we try to do this, our minds will still try to solve the problem because they do not like illogicality and insoluble problems. My wife likes crossword puzzles. She will go to sleep pondering the insoluble clue and wake up a few hours later with a cry of "I've got it!" Her mind, with its own brand of logic, has found the answer during her sleep. With illogicalities, though, we can try to put God in front of the irreconcilable, but it will not solve the problem. It is better to work a way through and find a solution. Now you may ask, "Where is all this leading us?"

There is a commonly misunderstood concept which says that God's ways cannot be found out by human logic. There is a difference, however, between things that are contrary to human logic and things that are beyond our understanding. In discussion with Job, God says that Job could not possibly understand all of his ways. He challenges Job and says, "Do you have an arm like God, and can you thunder with a voice like his?" (Job 40:9) The answer is in the negative. There is no way that Job can understand God's ways. They are beyond him in this area. We do not know exactly how God has made the world. We do not know how he put it together. We know that God is involved in some way but we cannot by our minds possibly work out all the details of the past, the countless millennia of human existence, let alone the existence of the universe. Advances in astrophysics have been astounding and have illuminated much regarding these origins, but the details are beyond our understanding.

However there is a difference between things that are beyond our understanding and things that are contrary to our understanding. For example, if it seems to human logic that an action is completely unloving and if this is followed by a statement that God has done it, then this appears illogical if God is love. To state that God is the author of all things, and then include within that authorship the Holocaust, the atrocities of Pol-Pot and the Rwandan genocide would seem to make nonsense of a God of love. We would be left with impossible conclusions. Either we must say, "God is love and he is not the author of these atrocities" or we must say , "These atrocities are his handiwork" and dispense with a God of love. It is impossible to have both. God has given us logic and reason to work things through and to work things out and he himself is not illogical.

This difference between those things that are beyond our understanding, and those things that are contrary to our understanding is actually very important. We can think God's thoughts after him. We can look at this world and discern and work things out. Newton and Einstein believed this. We can use our logic to determine results and conclusions. We can say that if A+B equals C, then A+B does not at the same time equal D, where D is different from C. We can use logic and reason in these kinds of ways. There will be areas that we will not fully understand because we do not have the mind of God himself. However, we can use our minds to understand that when God says that he is love, then actions that are unloving cannot originate from God.

This will become extremely important as we look more closely at the question of suffering. Does God cause suffering? Does God plan suffering to try us? Was God in control of the Holocaust? These are important questions that we will need to return to. It is important to keep before us that God is love before we approach these questions. Human logic and understanding has a reasonable grasp of what love is. The ability to make moral judgments comes from God himself. It is part of the image implanted in us. This is what St Thomas Aquinas was saying in his statement, "Reason in man is rather like God in the world."

Reason is part of the image that is within us. The reason and logic that God has given us is shared, in part, by the whole human race. It is purified and refined through our relationship with Christ. As we have the image of God, so we share in measure his logic and understanding. An appreciation of this will help us as we look more deeply at the problems caused by suffering.

CHAPTER 5

ARE WE FREE OR IN CHAINS?

—⁓—

We have considered the way God has given man his image and nature. This image was in man so that he could share God's world in joy and freedom. In the world he could be creative in his work and could look after the world as God's agent, filling it with beauty. He could use the raw elements from that world and mould them with his creativity so that they would be transformed into art, music, sculpture or whatever else he had a mind to make. If his talents lay in agriculture or horticulture, then abundant harvests and beautiful gardens would result. As he engaged in these pursuits, he would relate to God as Father and through joyful worship would fill the world with God's presence. Sadly this was not to be and instead of joyful freedom we more often have drudgery in work, or worse, actual slavery. The strong oppress the weak and the rich oppress the poor.

President Franklin Roosevelt said, "There never has been, there is not now and there never will be any race of people on earth fit to serve as masters over their fellow men." Freedom across the world is a very limited commodity. To express God's image in this world there needs to be freedom.

It is sad that social barriers in church life have impeded the gospel. Until this last generation, colour barriers in the American and South African churches have been major enemies to progress. The church has been slow to recognize the truth of what Thomas Fuller, a seventeenth century English writer observed, "Human blood is all the same colour."

There are many types of slavery, including that of children and sex slavery, often flourishing in impossible economic situations. Children lose their childhood to fight wars beyond their understanding. There may be slavery and exploitation to political systems or ideologies that remove basic human rights.

Closer to home, Paul writes at length about being slaves to sin. He emphasizes that slavery to sin can be impossible to break. This slavery to sin can be seen in many forms. One recent common addiction is that of internet pornography. People find it almost impossible to break free. The real problem is often not the pornography itself but what leads to the need to escape into pornography. It is the same with other conditions. Alcoholism and drug addiction can be tackled on the surface, by seeking to deal with the alcohol and drugs, but underlying problems may make cure difficult. The root causes need unearthing as well as the addictive habit. Later in the book I will be looking at some of these deeper problems in our lives. Rousseau has said, "Man was born free and everywhere he is in chains." Thank God there is freedom in Jesus.

Born Free?

There was a woman who was married to a mean and difficult man who pinned up rules all over the house. These told her to do certain things at certain times and were about such things as housekeeping, meals and so forth. Finally he died and was not missed over much! Later the woman married a wonderful man who was extremely good and kind to her. Some years later, as she cleared out an old trunk in the attic, she found the list of rules that her first husband had used. Looking over this, she made an amazing discovery. Everything the first husband had compelled her to do, she was now doing out of love for her second husband without even realizing it. She had moved from slavery into freedom but was actually doing the same things as before. But now her whole attitude and approach were completely different.

Love can only really exist where there is freedom. For love to be real it must not be forced. When I married my wife it was a free decision. In fact, there are grounds for annulling a marriage if one party did not freely agree to the contract. A marriage contract must be entered into voluntarily. When I married my wife it was a delight to say, "I will and I do."

As a psychiatrist for the elderly, I used often to be asked to assess whether people had capacity to make decisions. There are different elements to be considered in this process. Firstly is there understanding of what is being asked? Secondly can he or she fully understand the decision that is under consideration? Thirdly is there the ability to weigh up the consequences of acting or not acting on the decision being considered? Finally the person needs to be capable of expressing that decision clearly. Every decision under review requires a different level of capacity. They may well be able to decide they would like to live at home, but may not be able to manage their own finances. I need to gauge whether the person has the ability to make that choice, and to assess whether the effects of disease have compromised that ability.

What this process recognizes is that everybody should have the autonomy to make their own decisions once they have reached the age of majority. They should have freedom and others should not force them into making decisions. As Grotius, a Dutch statesman in the seventeenth century has said, "Liberty is that power we have over ourselves."

As parents, we have a responsibility to guide our children into the ways of freedom. There are few things more pitiful than to see adults in their mid-twenties totally tied to their parents and unable to make decisions for themselves. On the other hand, we do not expect a child of twelve or thirteen to be making decisions that really should be made for them by their parents. The challenge of parenthood is to be able to guide children in such a way that at appropriate stages in their maturity and development they are able to take certain decisions for themselves. God as a wise parent has set us free. Freedom is a reality and he does not want to force us by compelling us to do certain actions. Love cannot exist without this liberating kind of freedom. If God asks me to love him, I can only love him if I am free to do so. Love and freedom co-exist.

Dr Gordon was a famous minister of a church in Boston. One day while standing outside his church building he met a small boy carrying a rusty birdcage in his hands. Several little birds were anxiously fluttering around the cage as if they knew they had not long left to live. "Where did the birds come from?" he asked. The boy replied, "I trapped them out in the field." On further persistent questioning it transpired that the boy planned to take the birds home, play with them for a bit and feed them to an old cat.

Dr Gordon asked the boy how much it would cost to buy the birds. The boy was astonished. "Mister, you don't want those birds. They're just ordinary birds and they don't sing very well." Dr Gordon said, "I will give you two dollars for the cage and the birds." "All right" said the boy, "it's a deal. But you are making a bad bargain!"

The transfer was made and the boy sauntered down the street, whistling happily because of the two dollars in his pocket. Dr Gordon gently carried the cage behind the church building, released the catch on the rusty door and the liberated birds soared into the sky, singing joyously as they went. As he later explained in a sermon, "The boy said the birds couldn't sing very well, but when I released them from the cage they went singing away into the heavens."

There seems to have crept into much of our theology the idea that we are in some way controlled and the future is mapped out for us and we have no real freedom. Some have gone so far as to imply that we are either chosen or damned – effectively saying we have no choice. Such cannot be the case as God has chosen us and made us to be free. Indeed, we cannot live for God unless we are free to choose.

This freedom is an integral part of the Christian faith. Jesus said, "You will know the truth and the truth will make you free." He added emphatically, "So if the Son sets you free you will be free indeed." (John 8:32-33) In life we may have felt like those birds fluttering around in the cage powerless to escape and unable to sing. God opens the cage door, sets us free and we can go out singing. God revels in freedom and created it as a gift to us. Sadly in our lives we have become enslaved to sin and habits but Christ can set us free. He also wants to bring actual physical freedom to all who are currently enslaved in various parts of the world. Christ is a message of spiritual and physical freedom for the captives.

This freedom of course has been there from the very beginning when God created angels as free agents – free to worship God and to be glad servants of God. Freedom itself, however, always introduces the possibility of rebellion. Liberty to love opens up the possibility of liberty to rebel as they are opposite sides of the same coin. If I am free to marry, I am also free to not marry. If I am free to love God it follows that I am also free to rebel against him.

It seems entirely logical that God would create the angels with freedom so they could love and worship him. But it also seems logical to believe that the possibility of rebellion was there from the beginning. It would appear that many of the angels, following the example of Lucifer who was full of pride, turned and rebelled against God. The story of how this happened is hinted at in Isaiah 14:12-15. "How you have fallen from heaven, O star of the morning, son of the dawn! You have been cut down to the earth, you who have weakened the nations. But you said in your heart, 'I will ascend to heaven; I will raise my throne above the stars of God, and I will sit on the mount of assembly in the recesses of the north; I will ascend above the heights of the clouds, I will make myself like the Most High.' ... Nevertheless you'll be thrust down to Sheol, to the recesses of the pit."

Similarly in the book of Ezekiel it states regarding this same angel (Ezekiel 28:12), "You had the seal of perfection, full of wisdom and perfect in beauty. You were in Eden the garden of God; every precious stone was your covering." Then (verse 14) it says, "You were the anointed cherub who covers, and I placed you there. You were on the holy mountain of God; you walked in the midst of the stones of fire. You were blameless in your ways from the day you were created, until unrighteousness was found in you."

These passages indicate that Lucifer was created a beautiful, perfect and free agent. However Lucifer and his angels became proud and used their freedom to rise up against God himself. Following this, they were thrown down to earth and have been in rebellion ever since. It remains unclear as to exactly when this happened. Given the immense age of the universe (light from stars thirteen billion light years away is only now reaching us!) the possibilities here are enormous. It is also unclear exactly what powers they still have on the earth. Considering that Lucifer was close to God himself, the power base seems pretty strong.

In a similar way, mankind has been given freedom. In whatever way we may interpret the actual scene in the garden of Eden, it is quite clear that man and woman were created as reflections of God himself who gave them the gift of freedom. Given this choice they could choose to follow and obey God and enjoy companionship with him. They could walk with him in the garden in friendship and closeness or they could use their freedom to rebel against God their creator, leading to pain and separation. The story of the garden of Eden is a story of a choice made by man and woman together. They chose to rebel against God and go their own way rather than God's way. In the story Satan is involved as the deceiver and accuser, and he has continued in that role to this day.

This rebellion had serious consequences. As soon as rebellion comes in, slavery follows. In the garden they chose to be free from an ongoing relationship with God by choosing to break the single command he had given in the midst of fantastic lavish freedom. In doing this they became slaves to a law, the "law of sin and death." It would now be much more difficult, indeed impossible, to avoid further falling away from God. It is not long before the story turns to murder, rebellion and all kinds of evil, to the extent that God turned his back on an evil humanity, except for a few who were righteous at the time of Noah.

The story of the Old Testament is the story of God's desire to win back a people to love him and follow him in freedom. They would escape from the evil that surrounded them and would walk in love and fellowship with him. Following the flood of evil into the whole world and the physical flood in the time of Noah, God begins a recovery programme with Abraham, a man who was called a friend of God and who believed God. He and his household started a new journey of love with God. This was not just so that they would be blessed in themselves but rather that they would become avenues of blessing into the whole world.

As Abraham and his family experienced the presence and power of God, so they became able to pour that power into a world consumed by slavery to sin. The nation that Abraham would father would become an example to the other nations of how to live. It was intended that this would bring God's presence and life back into the world but sadly the opposite happened. The majority of the nation continued to use its freedom to rebel against God. Even under Moses, the nation was full of rebellion which led to 40 years wandering in the wilderness.

The book of Judges describes how righteous judges overcame sin and evil. Men like Gideon led the nation back towards God. Chaos took over when unrighteous judges took charge. Righteous kings like David pulled the people back on track but under bad kings the nation quickly drifted away from God leading to fragmentation, exile and hardship for the rebellious people of God. God's people had failed to show the world the nature of God. They had failed in their allotted task. Not just the nation, but also the world of that time suffered as a result. The exile purified the nation to an extent, but still patterns of sin remained.

It took the birth and life of Christ to begin a whole new movement of emancipation and through this all nations have been affected. We can now all be Abraham's children by faith in Christ Jesus. This liberty that we have is a very precious commodity. This is why Paul is keen that we should not sacrifice our freedom by going back under legal systems which are inappropriate reflections of the love of God. In most of his letters, Paul is at pains to make it clear that the liberty we have received through Christ, at such cost, must not be sacrificed for any reason.

If we are following Christ, we must follow him in freedom and take great care to maintain this liberty. If we lose it then we will end up going astray. We will become of little use if we allow sin to be a noose around us, or if we allow rules and regulations to tie us down rather than obeying Christ. We need to keep our energies for serving Christ and others, and to make sure that in the rat-race of life we prioritize those things which enhance communion with our Lover and the delight of walking with him in joy and closeness.

In the 1930s, at Louisiana State University there was a six-foot five inches tall heavyweight boxer called Alden Blakelock who had an extremely long reach. In the second round of one memorable fight, when he was pitted against a short stocky opponent, Blakelock let fly a furious right-hand punch which would have almost certainly been a knockout blow if it had landed. In a strategy to avoid the blow, his opponent had stepped in quickly and his head hit Blakelock's right elbow. This acted like a lever, adding power to Blakelock's punch, which then went right around the short man's head and ended up on Blakelock's own jaw. Stunned by his own blow, the fighter grasped the rope and started staggering round the ring before collapsing. He had managed to knock himself out!

This is what happens to many of us. We start off with freedom and enjoy it, but if we are not careful the world can pull us back into slavery, or we can knock ourselves out with our sin. We then become pretty useless until we find a way out. By going back to the cross we find deep in our hearts the reality and release that Christ has come to set us free. Like those birds released from the cage, we can enjoy the liberty that Christ has given us; we can enjoy it, and use it to bless the world.

The nation of Israel was supposed to bless the world, but largely failed. The judges and kings of Israel were supposed to bless the world but largely failed. Now, in these days we are called to rise up as a free people. Let us move out in the name of Christ, and in the power of Christ to bring his life to a dying and desolate world.

Whence The Chains?

Jean Pierre Camus, a French bishop in the seventeenth century said, "There are no galley slaves in the royal vessel of divine love – every man works his oar voluntarily." The intention of Christ is that we should be really free, and then to use this freedom to volunteer for action in his name. Paul writes simply, "But through love serve one another." (Galatians 5:13) Freedom for the Christian is not just being free from the penalty of sin; it is being free from its power, and it is enjoying liberty to be all that we were meant to be. It is to be released to fulfil our potential as we relate and move together with those who follow the same Lord. It is to restore the world to being the way it was intended to be.

Before we can fully explore these themes, we need to return for a while to the initial loss of freedom, and look more fully at how it occurred and at its implications. Whatever way in which we may interpret the early chapters of Genesis, it is clear that rebellion took place and this was followed by definite consequences. Following this rebellion in the garden of Eden the Lord God punished those involved; firstly the serpent, then the woman and finally the man. The Lord said to the serpent, "Because you have done this, cursed are you more than all cattle and more than every beast of the field; on your belly you will go, and dust you will eat all the days of your life. And I will put enmity between you and the woman, and between your seed and her seed; he shall bruise you

on the head, and you shall bruise him on the heel."
(Genesis 3:14-15)

The serpent or the enemy, the devil or the accuser,
will always be seeking to harm and damage humankind. This is because mankind bears the very image
of God himself which the devil cannot stand. For
this reason he is constantly seeking to destroy and
bring discord and damage to the human race. The
"enemy of our souls" declared perpetual war against
humanity. But even in this punishment of the serpent
we can begin to glimpse a promise present. Although
he might bruise our heel, in verse 15 it is written,
"He shall bruise you on the head." This can be seen
through the death of Christ many years later.

Many of the early Church Fathers took great
pleasure in recounting how Jesus had led the devil
on a chain. Others pictured him as being captured
on a fishhook. He was seen as being led along and
then finally destroyed through Christ's death on the
cross. Just as Satan tasted the sweetness of apparent
victory as Christ died on the cross, he suddenly
realized that he was completely undone and utterly
defeated. The death of Christ was a dramatic victory
over Satan as well as being the means of salvation
for the world. It was through Christ's death and
resurrection that the devil was defeated. Although
he is now a defeated foe, he refuses to accept defeat,
and we who follow the resurrected Christ need to
take authority over Satan and declare that the cross
and resurrection have robbed him of his power. He
is still active, but his power base has gone and his
ultimate destruction is certain.

To the woman God said, "I will greatly multiply your pain in childbirth; in pain you will bring forth children, yet your desire will be for your husband, and he will rule over you." (Genesis 3:16) Sometimes in the Old Testament it is not easy to distinguish between the natural consequence of an action, and actual punishment. It would seem most natural here to see that God is pointing out the consequences of the sin, and how that would affect womankind. He is not putting woman down and giving men permission to abuse women. Far from it! What he is saying is that relationships will be disturbed at all levels and as a result men will abuse women. Pain and discord, in the main, would characterize the relationship between the sexes rather than harmony.

Man would tend to dominate the woman from a position of greater physical strength. In today's world it is abundantly clear that the relationship between the sexes is not equal and harmonious. The woman is often demeaned by man and damaged physically, emotionally and sexually. In the Middle East in the time of Christ, a woman was generally condemned to an inferior position. Christ, however, elevated the status of women and was delighted to welcome them as privileged followers. It was to women that the first revelation of the resurrection was entrusted. In modern-day society in the West, woman does not hold her rightful and equal position. She is less protected now and more unsafe on the streets of England than, for example, thirty years ago. It seems that as people have largely abandoned Christian teachings and principles so threats and actual violence have increased against women causing them to be more vulnerable.

The worldwide increase in the sex slave trade is a horrifying example of the abuse of women. Likewise the removal of the rights of women in Afghanistan under the Taliban is another. Under this regime women were not allowed to work (except for a few in health services) or attend schools. They were not permitted to appear in public without a family member. They could be served only by females in shops. It was forbidden to play sports or enter sporting clubs. It was obligatory to wear a burqa covering them from head to toe, and if an inch of ankle showed they could be beaten on the spot. Their window on the world quite literally came from a three-inch-square opening in the burqa covered with mesh in front of their eyes. Cosmetics, brightly coloured clothing and high-heeled shoes were denied them. Access to the few female doctors was difficult, and they were the only ones permitted to treat women. They were not allowed to laugh loudly. Houses with female inhabit-ants had their windows painted over. Human rights of all kinds were horribly abused. What do these violations of basic human rights show us about the tendency that there is in man to abuse women?

Granted the above example is extreme, but is this tendency not widely prevalent in more miti-gated forms? Given the opportunity, man seems to use his abilities and his greater physical strength to subjugate woman and to keep her in a subordinate position. However, this tendency seems to be held in check where the teachings and example of Christ are followed. Christ honoured women and, following his example, Christian society has usually given women a higher place than they have in other cultures.

Turning now to the effects of this rebellion on the man we read, "Then to Adam he said 'Because you have listened to the voice of your wife, and have eaten of the tree about which I commanded you, "You shall not eat it", cursed is the ground because of you; in toil you will eat of it all the days of your life; both thorns and thistles it shall grow for you, and you will eat the plants of the field. By the sweat of your face you will eat bread, till you return to the ground, because from it you were taken. For you are dust, and to dust you shall return.'" (Genesis 3:17-19)

It is interesting to note that God declares that the ground is cursed, not man. Man is not cursed, but the ground will grow thorns and thistles. From this cursing of the ground, we can reasonably conclude that the world is not the way it should be. The world is out of order. Although there is tremendous beauty in the world there is also pain, discord, and the very environment itself seems at times to be in rebellion against the God of creation.

In the very act of rebelling against God, man fell prey to the enemy who was also in the garden. As the arch-enemy of God and of his image, man, he now held man close in his clutches. C S Lewis alludes to this in The Lion, the Witch and the Wardrobe. All would be bleak and frozen under the evil reign of the white witch. Under her sway all was dead and lifeless. The world was frozen and spring seemed to have passed away forever. Like Satan, she held the world in an icy grip. Only the lion, Aslan (a picture of Christ) could release the world from her icy embrace by his life-giving breath.

It is against this background that we need to understand what freedom really is. In the Bible we read that all humankind continued in this rebellion that had begun with Adam. What Adam did came upon the human race. St Augustine saw this sin being handed on through inheritance. In other words we were born in sin and this sin was handed on from generation to generation by means of inheritance. This is but one viewpoint. Others have suggested from a careful examination of Romans chapter 5, the following alternative. All of us sin in practice, in the same way as our forefathers, but this sinful tendency is not passed on to us by inheritance. We are all prone to rebellion and end up rebelling, but this is something for which we are responsible. This responsibility for our actions may be present from an early age, but we are not automatically sinful at birth, as suggested by St Augustine and those who follow him.

Sin does place chains around us and these chains lead to death. Liberty is stepping into freedom from the chains that bind us. We can then take hold of the tremendous creative potential of our lives. Christ brings us a freedom not only from the penalty of sin and its punishment, but also from its power. Through his death and resurrection Christ has announced liberty to the captives.

A poignant picture of this is given to us in the Old Testament where we read the story of Hosea, the prophet. God gave a strange request to Hosea to marry Gomer, a prostitute. Hosea knew his God and obeyed by taking Gomer in marriage. She subsequently gave him three children. Sadly in time Gomer went back to her old ways. She left Hosea's home where he had provided for her and went back onto the streets as a common prostitute. The story relates how Hosea went looking for her and found her in the slave market. He paid for her on the spot and brought her back under his own roof. It must have taken considerable courage to act like this in the eyes of all his friends and neighbours. Hopefully she behaved better afterwards. One wonders.

The story is used by God to illustrate his love for Israel. Even though Israel had been unfaithful like Hosea's wife and left him, God was willing to go to the extent of finding the slave in the slave market, paying for her and bringing her back. God was not ashamed to go public in his love and concern for the human race. On the cross, Christ hung in the public place and paid in his own blood the price to buy us back. Now we can belong to God again, despite our spiritual adultery. Christ has been to the slave market, broken the chains and set us free. He now calls us to "go public" and identify with him in his journey. This journey took Christ outside the city to a lonely hillside. We are called to identify with him, and to be willing to face the world's ridicule. "So let us go to him outside the camp, bearing his reproach. For here we do not have a lasting city, but we are seeking the city which is to come." (Hebrews 13:12-13)

CHAPTER 6

SUFFERING -WHO STARTED IT?

—ɱ—

In the early part of the nineteenth century an artist, Moritz Retzsch, who was also a chess player, painted a picture of a chess game where the players were a young man and his opponent was Satan. The young man moved the white pieces and Satan the black pieces. The issue was this: if the young man should win, he was to be forever free from the power of evil; should the devil win, the young man was to be his slave forever.

The artist evidently believed in the supreme power of evil for in his picture the devil was on the point of winning. Satan had just moved his queen and had announced a check-mate in four moves. The young man's hand hovered over his rook; his face was pale with foreboding and fear. His position seemed hopeless. The devil would win and the young man was to be a slave forever.

Chess players from all over the world viewed the picture. They all agreed with the artist that in the picture the devil was triumphant. One chess player, the great Paul Morphy, came to view the picture. Suddenly his hand paused and he could see a combination that everyone else had missed. He announced, "Young man, make that move!" The old master had discovered a combination that the creating artist had not considered. The young man now defeated the devil.

This is rather like the problem of suffering. It is as though the devil has made the master moves. Although the earth shines on the one hand with the grandeur of God, on the other, the earthquakes, the disasters, the Holocaust, and the presence of pervasive evil, show that the world is out of joint, and not what it should be. It is as though the devil has held the master moves. Like the chess player we seem to face imminent defeat. Our fate stares us in the face. Check-mate is round the corner. Satan seems to await his prey gleefully. "I have them now!" he thinks. "They will never find a way through all the pain and suffering." But wait a minute! Is there some move we have missed? Is there a hidden, not-thought-of combination that will yet give us a way out of the dilemma? I believe there is.

The atrocities of the twentieth century were worse than any previous century. It has been calculated that there were more martyrs for the Christian faith in the twentieth century, than in the previous nineteen combined together. People today are looking to Christians, as thinking believers, to supply answers to the major problems of the world. As twenty-first century believers we need to keep our feet on the ground and find some answers.

If we face the world and its mess without thought and prayer, we will end up as confused as everyone else and have little to offer others in their distress. We need to get our heads straight! George Herbert, a Church of England clergyman and poet of the seventeenth century said, "He that hath a head of wax must not walk in the sun." Suffering is like the scorching sun. We need to think, and think deeply, about the world and its problems, so that our heads are not wax and do not melt under the onslaught of the problems and suffering of life.

Many Christians believe that there are no answers to the problems of suffering and pain. Unbelievers, seemingly, have the upper hand and can mock the Gospel, because it appears to fail to provide satisfactory answers in this crucial area. The response that "suffering improves the character" is unconvincing. There are probably more people who are destroyed by troubles and pains than actually come through stronger as a result. Thomas Fuller, a seventeenth century English writer said, "If afflictions refine some, they consume others."

Some say that it is in identification with the afflictions of others that we will find our role and value. They point out examples like Father Damien and Mother Teresa. "Look at the love and sacrifice shown!" they may say. These examples are laudable. But this rather misses the point. The suffering is still there and remains unexplained. To find a role in sharing it and to help the sufferer is good, but to explain it to the doubter or infidel is another question. However we look at it, suffering is a major problem. It would seem as though in the pains and afflictions of life, Satan has us cornered. "Explain your loving God in the face of these problems." he taunts.

One of the interesting things about the issue of suffering is that it never seems problematic to the writers of the New Testament. We do not read in the pages of the New Testament that it was a problem to the disciples or the early church. There is no suggestion that it was an academic problem or a difficulty to be faced or puzzled over. They approached it in a completely different way. They saw diseases, pain and death as enemies to be overcome. They did not believe that they were sent to reason about the problem of suffering or even to empathize with those afflicted. Rather they understood that they were called to bring in the reign and Kingdom of God into the centre of the pains and afflictions and overcome them. Twelve and then 70 disciples were sent into the highways and byways of Israel with instructions to heal the sick, cure the blind, cast out the demons and preach the Kingdom of God. (Luke 9 and 10) As they went out in the name of Jesus, sickness vanished in their path. It is recorded several times of Jesus that he healed all who came to him. Suffering was not a problem to be understood: it was an enemy to be overcome.

Several times in John's Gospel, Jesus talks about the devil as "the ruler of this world." (John 12:31, 14:30, 16:11) He is stating in this that there is another force in this world, the devil, who is ruler of this world. We do not talk in these days much at all about

Satan, or the devil. Even less do we refer to him as the ruler of this world. Jesus seems quite happy to use this terminology. John in his first letter repeats the message like this, "We know that we are of God, and that the whole world lies in the power of the evil one." (1 John 5:19) The "cosmos" or whole world order is in the evil one's domain. Hostility is expressed against Christians. It is certainly expressed against God. The world is "in the power of the evil one."

It is interesting the way in which Jesus is tempted. "Again, the devil took him to a very high mountain, and showed him all the kingdoms of the world and their glory and he said to him, 'All these things I will give you if you fall down and worship me.' Then Jesus said to him, 'Go, Satan! For it is written, "You shall worship the Lord your God and serve him only"'. Then the devil left him." (Matthew 4:8-11) Jesus does not here challenge the authority of the devil to offer him the kingdoms of the world and all that is within them. All he says to the devil is, "You shall worship the Lord your God, and serve him only." That the devil is allowed to offer the kingdoms of the world to Jesus Christ the Son, is not called into question.

The disciples and the early church believed this world to be an evil place. An evil being inhabits it and his ways are evident in this world. This would fit in with the biblical record of the enemy, or the devil, being cast down to earth. He tempted Adam in the garden and has been unleashed in the world ever since. The death and resurrection of Christ have given him his marching orders but until that victory is enforced by the storm troops of the church he clings on.

In the early church this idea of Christ being victorious over Satan was understood clearly. Christ had come into the world and through his perfect life was demonstrating a new way to the whole of humanity. As Adam had brought all into death, so through Christ all now could come into life. Christ in his incarnation and life demonstrates perfect manhood and through his death and resurrection restores humanity to its initial calling and relationship with its creator. Faced with persecution by the Roman Empire, believers could take comfort in the knowledge that Christ had won the ultimate victory.

Many of the early believers were slaves. The idea that Christ had been offered as a ransom for their release from bondage to Satan could be readily understood, given their position in life. Christ with his own blood had paid the price to buy them back from the devil. Satan thought he was victorious with Christ hanging on the cross and gloated over his apparent victory. Because he thought he was the victor and in control, the resurrection must have been a rude awakening shock. Having dreamt of gaining all and planning meticulously for success, he found himself utterly defeated. The blood of Christ had paid the price for Satan's power over individuals to be broken. They could now be free and exult in their new relationship with God as Father. With God's power they could begin to set others free.

The disciples in the early church believed they could overcome the problems of pain and suffering through the power of Christ. The sick were healed where Jesus went and the disciples walked. The ill and suffering were healed as they came to Jesus and he touched them or spoke a healing word. In Acts we read that the sick were also made well where Peter's shadow fell on them. The only time in the New Testament that there is even a hint of suffering causing a problem is in John chapter 9. As the disciples see a man who was born blind they asked the pertinent question. "Rabbi, who sinned, this man or his parents, that he would be born blind?" Jesus proceeds to cure the man.

The response of Jesus before he does this has been variously understood. The traditional understanding has seemed to place the responsibility for the man's blindness on God's doorstep by more or less stating that God caused him to be born blind, so that Jesus the Son could then come along and heal him. Although the passage has been understood this way in the main, it does seem unsatisfactory for all kinds of reasons. It seems that God is playing around with a man's eyesight just so that Jesus, his Son, can come along to heal him and prove a point.

There are much better explanations and understandings of the text. (John 9:2-4) The passage can be translated in either of the following manners depending on how one chooses to punctuate the unpunctuated Greek, and also depending on the exact translation of the Greek words. It can read in this way. "Jesus said, 'It was not that this man sinned or his parents, but that the works of God might be manifested in him. We must work the works of him who sent me while it is day.'" Jesus is saying we must work the works of God to overcome the sickness and the blindness. An alternative translation would read, "Jesus said, 'It was not that this man sinned or his parents. But let the works of God be manifested in him.'"

Jesus is attacking the blindness. He is not in any way seeking to explain its origin. That is not his intention. Either of these alternatives is viable, and neither attributes the causation of the blindness to God. It would in any case be unsound theology to develop a belief in God's causing blindness or any other physical problem from a single verse in the Bible. Nowhere else in the New Testament do we get the suggestion that God causes pain and disease. Rather we are to understand from the New Testament that the disciples saw pain, sickness and death as evils to be overcome. They were the evidence that the ruler of this world was alive and active.

The suffering was the result of the evil one's presence in the world. Satan, although vanquished, holds on tenaciously and needs to be forced out. This happens as the Kingdom of God advances. Jesus said, "From the days of John the Baptist until now the Kingdom of heaven suffers violence, and violent men take it by force." (Matthew 11:12) The Kingdom of God is advancing, and it is advancing through force. This force is not physical, but is the result of Christians worshipping, praying, proclaiming the good news and working together to see evil overthrown. As we do our part, so God does his part and puts the enemy to flight.

As we recognize the Kingdom of God among us, we are able to take a stand against the pain of this world, with the power and presence of Christ. As the Kingdom of God advances, so the kingdom of the enemy is thrown down. From the account of sin and its entry into the world, (Genesis 3) it seems clear that the world is not the way it should be. This world is out of synchrony with its creator. It is in this light that we are to see natural disasters. Earthquakes such as the recent one in Bam in Iran show that things are not the way that God intended. Children being born deformed or with major genetic defects is not God's intention in this world.

Many will ask about these and other similar tragedies, "How can you see the hand of God in this?" That question is so deeply built into our psyche that it appears to come quite automatically. I am not sure we should even look for the hand of God in this. Another hand has done this! It seems better to attribute these disasters and pain to the work of the "ruler of this world." If we try and somehow attribute a disease such as Huntington's Chorea to God's intention, then we will surely become hopelessly unstuck in our thinking about God.

It is much easier and I believe more appropriate to blame this on "the ruler of this world" who is alive and active on planet Earth. If he is indeed ruling on the earth, as the Bible clearly states, then his handiwork will be seen in the way the world malfunctions. This may be seen in the recent tsunami in the Indian Ocean of 26 December 2004 as well as in earthquakes and genetic illness. It may not always be easy to see

Satan as the immediate cause, but if one accepts that he is an active agent, then he may be seen as the ultimate cause of the problems.

In stating forcibly the role of Satan in the world today, can we still talk about God reigning? The Psalms in particular talk much about God's reign in the earth. It is absolutely clear that God will bring everything to completion, and the enemy and his forces await a fiery destruction. (Revelation 20:10) It is equally true that God has the power to end things at any time. But as 2 Peter 3:8-9 makes clear, he is delaying action to provide opportunity for repentance. This delay allows the enemy to continue his evil schemes, except that we have as the church the authority to command him to move on.

Why Is The Pain So Bad?

Adoniram Judson, missionary to Burma spent seven years in tremendous hunger and deprivation. He experienced almost incredible mistreatment. As a result, for the rest of his life, he carried ugly marks made by the chains and shackles which had bound him. When he returned to America, his face shone with a supernatural light. As he was passing through the city of Stonington, Connecticut, a young boy playing near the seashore noted his arrival. He had never before seen such a light shining on any face. He ran up to a minister to ask who the stranger was. The minister hurried back with him but then became so involved in conversation with Judson that he forgot all about the young boy.

Many years later that boy, who could never forget the impression that wonderful face had made upon him, became a famous preacher. In his memoirs he wrote a chapter called "What a boy saw in the face of Adoniram Judson." The supernatural light he had seen in Judson's face as a child had changed the young boy's life. The pain and persecution endured as a result of voluntary service to Christ can bring unexpected and quite remarkable results. "Does God know what is going on in my life?" I wonder if Judson asked this. Did he question, "Why doesn't God do something about all my troubles and pain?"

Pain and suffering in our lives may come as a result of actions of those we thought were our friends. One of the deepest and most painful wounds may come from hurt experienced in church life. It is extremely sad when Christians fall out and separate from each other. When Christian leaders squabble and fight, the damage in lives can be immense. Those closest to us have the capacity to cause us the greatest emotional pain and sorrow. "Friendly fire" can be deadly in its effects. Many of us involved in church leadership and counselling will have spent hours with individuals who have felt devastated by pain caused by division in the church and the resulting separation from long-standing friends.

The beautiful thing about God is that he has come down to where we are and has shown us that he cares deeply for us. He has experienced our pains and trials. The film, The Passion of The Christ shows powerfully the suffering that Christ went through. He identifies with us in our pain. He endured suffering and pain and acute agony beyond description. Not only was the physical pain intense, but the mental torture of experiencing what it felt like to be cut off from God his Father, as he bore all the sin of the world, was overwhelming. "It is with his stripes we are healed." (Isaiah 53:5) Christ's broken and bruised body created a way through for us to find life. To the individual in pain, we can at least say, "Christ knows what you're going through, because he has been through it himself."

The book of Hebrews tells us that he has become a High Priest for us. As the person confesses his or her need, the priest can understand and identify with the pain, trials and torment of the person. Jesus is the perfect priest who can understand and identify with us. Hebrews 4:15 states, "For we do not have a high priest who cannot sympathize with our weaknesses, but one who has been tempted in all things as we are, yet without sin." Christ can identify with our pain and suffering. He has been there and knows what it is like through his experiences on earth and on the cross. He knows and understands the score.

If in the cross Christ identifies with our pain, in his resurrection he proclaims his power over it. In his resurrection appearances to his disciples he makes it clear that they, and the whole church which follows, are to have his authority. The disciples had observed this in the power of Christ over sickness, death and the demonic. Christ, before he left this world spoke to his followers in these words. "All authority has been given to me in heaven and on earth. Go therefore and make disciples of all the nations." (Matthew

28:18-19) Jesus is saying here that as authority has been given to him, so he now hands this over to the church. It is fully realized when the Holy Spirit invades the New Testament church coming as tongues of fire upon them. As Christ loved the world, so his church is called to move into the world and begin to help overcome its pains and sorrows. That is his mandate. As they made disciples of all nations, so the forces of darkness and evil would be pushed back. The job would be incomplete however until the good news had reached every nation. Then the King would return. (Matthew 24:14)

The questions arise. Why then is suffering and pain still such a major problem? Why is the world not changed or transformed by the power of Christ? Why do the problems still exist? These are very reasonable questions. Here is a story of the conversation between the Pope of the time and St Thomas Aquinas. The Pope was counting out his worldly possessions. The medieval church had become very rich. As St Thomas approached him, the Pope said, "Ah, Thomas, no longer can we say 'silver and gold have I none,'" to which Thomas is reputed to have replied, "Yes, that is true. But neither can we say 'In the name of Jesus Christ of Nazareth, rise up and walk.'" (Acts 3:6)

The church sadly had lost its power and authority. Materialism had crept in and the power had gone.The same is true today where the church, in general, is in a parlous state. The power is missing. The passion is gone. The splits and disunity have robbed us of our inheritance. Where churches tend to be territorial, the progress of the individual congregation or denomination can be seen as more important than the growth and development of the church as a whole. We need to remember that when we meet Christ the key question to be answered is whether we have been true and faithful servants. I do not think we will be questioned about our denominational affiliation! In the early chapters of the book of Acts the church is moving as one body. There is an absence of competition. The Holy Spirit in these same chapters, significantly, is noted for his powerful presence!

In some places in the world where the church comes together in large bodies, God seems to honour the unity achieved by visiting us once again with his manifest presence. Such moves demand, first of all, humility and the willingness to lay aside our divisions. In our current divided and sometimes hostile state towards one another, it seems small wonder that the power is missing, and the suffering, sick and hurting carry on with their needs unmet.

In other places, where the church is lacking physical resources and consequently more desperate to find God's help, amazing miracles take place. Such happenings should actually be the norm. In these places when they pray fervently together, then situations are transformed. It is clearly documented that the sick are healed and the dead are raised. In the midst of desperate poverty and families orphaned through AIDS, life is renewed as God touches situations with his compassion and power as the whole church moves as one. How we long to see this happen in the West! Jesus came to invade the kingdom of darkness, and this invasion is made real by his followers as we take that authority into our hands and stand together in his name to overcome the forces of evil.

A further question is often raised. Why doesn't God intervene to stop the suffering and pain? One of the difficulties here is trying to grapple with what in reality we are asking God to do. God is a personal God with defined characteristics. We have spent time discussing his primary characteristic, emphasized in the Bible, which is "God is love." God is also just and holy. Sin cannot abide the radiance of his holy presence. Those who failed to comprehend the burning holiness of the divine presence in the Old Testament discovered the consequences to their cost. When the ark of God was being moved back towards Jerusalem, Uzzah touched it and perished as a result. (2 Samuel 6:6) Between us and the glory and majesty of God's holy presence must come an intermediary otherwise none of us could stand in his presence. We would all be burnt up in his awesome light and power.

It is likewise when we invite God to intervene directly in our world. In asking him to move in, which of us could withstand the consequences? God has wisely chosen in the new era initiated by Christ not to operate in this direct way except on certain rare occasions. Rather he has delegated his authority to the church, which will, in obedience to him, get the job done. I believe this is why the church has been given the job of taking the gospel to the ends of the earth. As Christ's ambassadors we are able to act in love. God is not willing that anyone should be destroyed. The Bible teaches us, "The Lord is not slow about his promise as some count slowness, but is patient towards you, not wishing for any to perish but for all to come to repentance." (2 Peter 3:9) He is holding back the Second Coming of Christ to give as many as possible the opportunities to repent.

There will come a time when he will intervene more directly. The Bible is clear that Christ will come again in the future. Now, though, in the present age he is withholding his hand for a very good reason. He wants all to repent and all to come to know the truth. He is not wishing that any should perish. Jesus has said the gospel will go to the ends of the earth and then the end will come. Before that, his gospel is to be preached to all nations. The aim of preaching the gospel, of course, is so that men will turn from evil and the ways of Satan, and come into the joy and gladness of knowing that they are children of God.

In order to carry out this task, the church is called not only to speak out the Word of God, but also to act it out in deeds of loving kindness, and miracles that demonstrate the power of God in our midst. The work of the church is not words only, but words and works and wonders done in the power of the Holy Spirit. However, while we live in an evil and corrupt world, it is not surprising that evil and corruption touch us at some points in our lives. Whatever our spiritual state, we share the same human condition. "For he causes his sun to rise on the evil and the good, and sends rain on the righteous and the unrighteous."(Matthew 5:45) The rain falls on the just as well as the unjust. Problems come into all of our lives.

There are pains and trials that are part of human existence. These tend to affect all in a fairly indiscriminate manner. They are part of our human experience as we live in a fallen world. We need to expect that suffering and pain will come into our lives because we live in a world that is basically out of connection with its creator. If we think this way, it will help us when difficulties come, and in the midst of the pain, there will be places and times where life and light and power break through.

As well as this general suffering, direct hostility is shown against Christians. It is part of the attack waged against God by the evil one in the world. The reign and work of the devil in the world are clearly evident and will affect us in sickness, in pain and in suffering. It will impact us in genetic malformations, in inherited diseases, in earthquakes, and in volcanoes: it will disturb and sadden us through the Holocaust, the Rwandan genocide and similar atrocities.

Coping With Really Bad Pain

I have enjoyed reading many of the excellent historical novels of Sir Walter Scott. I was interested to note the contrast between himself and Lord Byron. Both experienced lameness but their responses were quite different. Byron was made bitter by his illness and never went into a public place without thinking about his disability, so much so that much of the colour and joy of life were lost to him. Scott, on the other hand, never complained about his disability even to his closest friend. It should not surprise us that Sir Walter Scott should have received a letter from Byron which included this sentence: "Scott, I would give my fame to have your happiness."

Trials and pains come because we live in a broken and hostile world. None of us can expect to live lives free from hardship. Faced with difficult experiences we can react like Scott or Byron. That choice is ours. Suffering is of two kinds. Firstly, is that which is part of everyday existence which is unavoidable and occurs because we live in a hostile and broken world. There is a second kind of suffering which Jesus points out in these words, "And he who does not take his cross and follow after me is not worthy of me. He who has found his life will lose it, and he who has lost his life for my sake will find it."(Matthew 10:38-39)

Jesus calls us to serve and take up a cross and follow him. It was that cross that drove Damien to the Island of the Lepers. It was that cross that drove Mother Teresa to Calcutta. This cross is voluntary. When we take it up we are saying, "I am willing to suffer for the sake of Christ." As we reflect on these selfless lives laid down in sacrificial service, these lives become our inspiration.

Let us summarize the two ways we can respond to suffering. The first way is by enduring and overcoming it, rather than allowing it to destroy us. I am constantly inspired by a friend of mine called Ray. Despite over thirty years of pain, he does not complain. Often he has to spend long periods of time at home, unable to go out because of extreme pain made worse on movement. In the midst of severe discomfort he turns his attention towards Christ. He reads very widely, and shares his insights through his tape ministry and as I write this book I am indebted to him for several valuable insights. That is a way of enduring and overcoming. In trials and difficulties we can dig deep and find fresh resources. The Psalms of David are full of the strength he finds in God in the midst of being pursued by those out to kill him.

The following story illustrates the hidden resources we can find when it seems we are in a desert place. One of the hottest regions on earth is alongside the Persian Gulf where little or no rain falls. Yet over the years many people have lived here by the sea. This is because springs of fresh water break out of the seabed. They discovered that fresh water could be obtained by diving. The diver takes a leather bag and dives to the bottom of the sea and quickly places the bag over the freshwater waterspout, before tying the bag and returning to the surface. Springs of fresh pure water are discoverable in the depths. As we go through painful trials, we may well find springs of water in the midst of them. This is what my friend Ray has discovered. Suffering, approached the right way, does release springs of water and sweetness.

It can also make others bitter and cause them to turn their back on God. As Thomas Jefferson said, "Grief drives men into serious reflection." The results of this reflection may move a person to go in one of two directions, as illustrated by the lives of Scott and Byron. Our mental approach when faced with suffering is all-important. Thomas Kingsley, an English novelist, said "Pain is no evil unless it conquer us." Through pain and trials we can emerge stronger through finding fresh springs in the depths, or we can go under completely. Both are possible.

A second way of responding to suffering is to identify with it. This is what it means to "take up the cross and follow Christ." It means voluntary identification with the pain and difficulties of others. It involves willingness, if necessary, to pay the ultimate price of martyrdom for the sake of Christ. A vivid illustration of this was given to the world in the late nineteenth century. At that time literally scores of young people boarded boats to go to West Africa with the Gospel. They took their coffins with them. Life expectancy was less than one year in West Africa for those unused to the diseases and climate. The vibrant church in West Africa today is a visible tribute to their sacrifice. Soren Kierkegaard, a nineteenth century Danish philosopher and theologian stated, "A tyrant dies and his rule ends; the martyr dies and his rule begins."

In the reign of the Roman emperor Nero, there was a fearless band of soldiers known as the Emperor's Wrestlers. In the amphitheatre they defended the arms of the emperor against all challengers. A more courageous group of warriors was scarcely known. Through the courts of Rome would ring the cry, "We, the wrestlers, wrestling for thee, O Emperor, to win the victory for thee and the victor's crown." When the Imperial army went to fight in France, this band of wrestlers was known to be particularly brave and loyal and was led by the centurion Vespasian. Many of them had become

Christians. Nero sent a message to Vespasian instructing him that all Christians must be killed.

The message was received in the middle of winter when the soldiers were camped on the shore of a frozen lake. It was with a sinking heart that the centurion read the emperor's message. Vespasian called the soldiers to him. "Is there any among you who is a Christian? If so let him step forward!" Forty wrestlers immediately stepped forward, respectfully saluted, and stood to attention. He had not imagined that so many of his best soldiers would be Christians. Vespasian gave them till nightfall to change their minds. The question was then asked a second time. Again the forty wrestlers stepped forward.

Vespasian pleaded with them but to no avail. Finally he said, "The command of the emperor must be obeyed. I am going to ask you to march out on to the lake. I will have to leave you to the mercy of the elements." The forty wrestlers were stripped and marched to the middle of the lake. As they marched they sang, "Forty wrestlers, wrestling for thee, O Christ, to win for thee the victory and for thee, the victor's crown." Throughout the long hours of the night Vespasian stood, watching. As morning drew near one soldier gave up and crept quietly towards the fire. In his suffering he had renounced his Lord.

Finally, clear from the darkness came a song. "Thirty-nine wrestlers wrestling for thee, O Christ, to win for thee the victory and for thee the victor's crown." Vespasian looked at the figure crawling towards the fire. He could bear it no longer. Off came his own helmet and clothing and he ran onto the ice crying, "Forty wrestlers, wrestling for thee, O Christ, to win for thee the victory and for thee the victor's crown."

To be a martyr is one thing, but to share the suffering and pain of a broken humanity on a constant and consistent basis, may take even greater courage. Samuel Rutherford, a Scottish minister of the seventeenth century said, "Whenever I find myself in the cellar of affliction, I always look about for the wine." And, "Jesus Christ came into my prison cell last night and every stone flashed like a ruby." He was finding out the glorious reality that God is no man's debtor. What was lost materially by being in prison for his Lord was more than recompensed by the glory of Christ's presence. Voluntary imprisonment for Christ has brought tremendous blessing through what has been written there over the centuries. How much poorer we would be without Paul's letters from various prison cells! The world would be greatly impoverished without John Bunyan's Pilgrim's Progress also written from a prison cell.

Voluntary suffering is an incandescent flame that lights our own path. Von Hugel, an English twentieth century philosopher said, "Devoted suffering is the only pure form of action." William Penn, founder of Pennsylvania stated, "No pain, no palm. No thorn, no throne." Deitrich Bonhoeffer who was martyred under the Nazis explained, "A Christian is someone who shares the suffering of God in the world." Those who voluntarily suffer for Christ enrich the world and they themselves seem to enjoy a special closeness to Christ which the rest of us envy.

What can be concluded from this brief study of suffering? Firstly, that suffering and pain are not God's intention for this world. Secondly, they are the evidence of a world out of synchrony with its creator. Thirdly, damage and trauma are the results of the presence of the "ruler of this world" or Satan. Fourthly, these things may affect Christian and non-Christian alike. Fifthly, the church has a mandate to overcome suffering and pain through its relationship with Christ. Sixthly, wherever the church unites together in love and prayer, pains and difficulties can be overcome. The victory however is incomplete. Greater success will be achieved, but some will only be seen when Christ returns. Finally, if we bear pains and trials we may become stronger – although not always. There are springs of living water to be found in the midst of even the darkest experience.

Finally, suffering is of two types. One is that which affects all mankind. The other is the suffering that Christ talks about when he asks us to take up the cross and follow him. As we voluntarily endure the pain of the cross, or even martyrdom itself, the world looks upon us astonished and sees there the light and life of Jesus.

CHAPTER 7

CAN THE WORLD BE CHANGED?

—《W—

It must have been the most profoundly amazing experience to be there on that first Easter Sunday morning. John and Peter are running as fast as they can to get to the tomb. Mary and the other women had said it was empty. What could have happened? Where was the body? Had it been stolen? Who had the power to roll away that gigantic stone? It was bad enough for their friend to die in such a horrific way, and now this! John is fitter and gets there first and pauses outside. Something amazing has happened. No earthly force could have rolled the huge stone such a distance. The trees and the ground look as if an earthquake has shaken the place violently. What on earth is going on? As he stands there in thought outside the open cave a completely fresh idea begins to form in his mind. "I wonder if it is possible," he muses.

Peter meanwhile has arrived panting and rushes straight in. He lifts up the limp grave clothes, trying to work out where the body is. John comes in and he knows. Everything suddenly begins to fall into place. This is what was meant to happen. He understands. I wonder what his first words were to Simon Peter. "Simon," he gasps, "do you know what has happened? He's alive! He has risen. Do you remember he said that three days later he would rise again? It's happened, Simon. It's all true. It has all been worth it. He will meet us again. Simon, he will forgive you! Besides, it wasn't just you. We all let him down."

Filled with joy and amazement, they race back to the others to tell of the wonderful events. Mary is sobbing in the garden as if her heart will break. Through the tears she peers into the tomb and is startled to see two angels "Woman why are you weeping?" they ask. Mary is confused. She is missing Jesus terribly. He had given her fresh hope in life and now he is not only gone but his body has disappeared and she is distraught. From behind her, another voice says the same thing, "Woman why are you weeping?"

She turns round thinking it is the gardener and that he has moved the body. Still distressed and eyes streaming with tears, she asks where the body is. He just simply says, "Mary" and her heart misses a beat. It can't be. It couldn't possibly be! But it is. She can't see properly, but she would know that voice anywhere. That was the voice that she had first heard in the midst of her life of misery, three years before. Everything is going to be all right. He was back again. Joy fills her heart and she rushes to grab hold of Jesus, for fear he would disappear again.

The resurrection of Jesus Christ dramatically changed the lives of those struck down by grief. It would slowly dawn on his followers that it was not just they who had been changed by the dramatic events. Everything was now different. The whole world order had changed. Death was not the end; it was just a stage on the journey.

Christ had triumphed over death and the grave. He had also defeated all his enemies. Satan himself was a defeated foe, although he had imagined a complete victory when he saw Jesus hanging on the cross. He thought he had scored the winning goal but it turned out to be an own goal. The death and resurrection of Christ had dealt him a deadly blow forever. Although vanquished he still refuses to accept defeat and continues to plague the world with his rearguard action. The church now has the responsibility, given by Jesus himself, to advance against him and bring into reality the victory that has been won.

With the resurrection a new day dawned. The disciples, in the space of a generation, turned the world upside down. (Acts 17:6) They were re-commissioned and given the authority of Christ. Where he had reigned, they would now take over. Jesus Christ had authority over sickness, pain and death. He had walked on water and fed the multitudes with a few loaves and some fish. He had moved the demons on with a word. Now the followers of Christ inherited all of this. They might have few possessions but there was no inheritance to equal this.

The resurrection heralded the hope of renewal for the whole of creation. This would not just be felt in the human sphere in terms of changed lives; it would be felt in the whole created order. The "evangelion" or good news was for the whole of creation. What was lost in the fall of Genesis could now be reclaimed. The land could rejoice under new ownership. The people of the new order, living in new communities, could bring newness and freshness to the earth. Every area of human endeavour could throb with the heartbeat of new life. The image of God could be seen in every corner of the globe.

This is the new order that Christ has come to introduce. He has brought individual salvation and eternal life for the believer but this is only part of what he has done. Christ has come to transform society. It is not a matter of waiting quietly in a corner until we are called upwards. It is not just "Pie in the sky when we die." It is indeed, "Cake on the plate while we wait!" We do not need to wait passively to receive all that is ours in the after life. We can enjoy the gifts of Christ in this life and bring his kingdom and blessing into this world now.

Christ has risen and now he wants to bring the world back to himself. The kingdom of Christ is invading the kingdom of darkness. This is happening in our world today. The power of Christ is being demonstrated in the different continents of the world. In India, in Korea, in South America, and in sub-Saharan Africa there are large population movements in the name of Christ. The gospel is spreading through China like wildfire. In many of these countries, there has been an explosion of commitment to mission abroad. The developing world is at the forefront of world mission. The Back to Jerusalem movement of the Chinese church, the missionary spirit of the Korean church, and the Brazilian and South American mission movements are astounding in their vision and zeal.

I have always loved to be involved in mission. I was deeply challenged at the age of eighteen to follow Christ by listening to George Verwer, the founder of Operation Mobilization. One of the times I enjoyed most was in Southern Italy in 1973. A team of thirteen of us travelled around in the back of a rickety old bread van and slept on hard church floors. There were times where we needed to believe God in faith for our next meal. Those two months were a highlight in my own experience. One of my most precious possessions is the Italian text of John's Gospel chapter 3 verse 16. It was given to me by a twelve-year-old girl Paula, who became a Christian at that time. At the end of the two months we wanted to stay in Italy. I do not think I have ever since known the depth of fellowship that we experienced at that time.

In Belfast, Northern Ireland, the church has been so encouraged by having a Brazilian couple over the last two years. Sergio and Anna have given us such a thrust forward in mission. It has been a privilege to co-operate with them in their mission plans and to join them on mission in Europe. The church is on the move. Christ has come to bring reconciliation into every area. The resurrection of Christ has begun a process of bringing new life into our lives and also into the whole of the created order. But the process will not be complete before the return of Christ.

In Romans 8:18-23 Paul says, "For I consider that the sufferings of this present time are not worthy to be compared with the glory that is to be revealed to us. For the anxious longing of the creation waits eagerly for the revealing of the sons of God. For the creation was subjected to futility, not willingly, but because of him who subjected it in hope that the creation itself also will be set free from its slavery to corruption into the freedom of the glory of the children of God. For we know that the whole creation groans and suffers the pains of childbirth together until now; and not only this, but also we ourselves, having the first fruits of the Spirit, even we ourselves groan within ourselves, waiting eagerly for our adoption as sons, the redemption of our body."

Sometimes in interpreting passages like this, we are not sure how much of this is for now and how much refers to the future. The creation is seen as longing for the liberty of the sons of God. We who follow Christ are sons and daughters of God! We are looking forward to a new age when our bodies will be set free from their earthly shackles. Even now where the church is strong and united, new life is invading not only the spiritual but also the natural dimension. It has been amazing to observe the experience of Christians in Guatemala. After they came together to pray earnestly, they found to their astonishment that their harvests increased dramatically. Pictures may be seen of carrots as big as a man's arm! The "Transformations" video series shows this as well as many well-documented examples of community transformation. This increase in their crops seemed to follow directly upon their new spiritual unity in Christ after they earnestly prayed together.

It is still not known how much our environment could be changed if Christians united together. Much of the change in creation that Paul mentions above may not be relegated to the future kingdom, but may be obtainable now. The creation is certainly "in bondage to decay." However, Christians working together in power and unity may bring change that has not before been imagined. The resurrection of Christ sets in motion a whole new movement and a whole new order. A new humanity comes under his lordship.

Christ is interested in bringing reconciliation into all things. The key is man. Man is like a gateway between God and the physical environment. The physical environment finds reconciliation as it is brought back to God through the mediation of man. We are very special in God's purposes. Paul talks about this in 2 Corinthians 5:17. "Therefore, if anyone is in Christ, he is a new creature; the old things passed away, behold new things have come. Now all these things are from God, who reconciled us to himself, through Christ, and gave us the ministry of reconciliation; namely that God was in Christ reconciling the world to himself."

God reconciles us to himself and aims that through us there will be a transformation process, which will begin to set free the world from bondage and decay. Much of this awaits completion at the Second Coming of Christ. What is not clear is how much of this can be seen in advance if the church really gets moving. This is why it is essential that differences that separate us are overcome, and we work together in co-operation, because we do not yet know how much God might do through us. The things that are being seen today in Guatemala are small examples of what God can do, and will do, when given the opportunity by Christians working together in love.

This love needs to be expressed in all kinds of ways. In the New Testament era it was one of the main aims of the church to care for the poor. Paul spent much of his energy arranging for collections to be made for the poor Christians in Jerusalem. (2 Corinthians 9 for example) The early church at one stage took over the responsibility for providing for the poor in Rome. Today the work of Tearfund and many other Christian organizations have been at the forefront in bringing practical help and employment opportunities to the poor in many countries. Clear objectives have been set to make poverty history. For love to be real it needs to be practical. James reminds us of this. "But prove yourselves doers of the Word, and not merely hearers who delude themselves."(James 1:22) Jesus calls us to mission, but this involves taking responsibility for the environment as well as practical love and care for the poor. We are called to be heralds of a whole new order.

Is Transformation Possible?

Tahiti has always been a fascinating island. Small wonder! Tropical climate, lush surroundings and overwhelming warmth and hospitality. In 1788 the "Bounty" sailed to Tahiti. Having sailed 27,000 miles, the crew rather enjoyed being on the beautiful island. But then the ship set sail on 4 December 1789 for the second leg of its journey. A little more than three weeks later near the island of Tonga the crew, led by first mate Fletcher Christian, staged a mutiny against Captain William Bligh, under whom they claimed to have suffered inhuman treatment.

After the mutiny Fletcher Christian and those with him settled on a small volcanic island called Pitcairn on 23 January 1790. However shortly after arriving on the island everything seemed to go wrong. It became a kind of "Lord of the Flies" establishment. Despite Fletcher Christian's efforts to maintain peace, the Polynesian men (who had accompanied the mutineers) revolted against the English oppressors in 1790. Several mutineers were killed, among them Fletcher Christian.

In 1800 Alex Smith, the only surviving mutineer, discovered a Bible in a chest from the "Bounty" which had floated to the island. He opened the Bible and began to read it and as a result he began holding regular Sunday services and teaching the Christian faith in the settlement. His gentleness and tolerance enabled the small company to thrive, and peace was restored to Pitcairn. In 1808 the passengers on an American sailing ship "Topaz" called to the island and they found it a place full of peace and harmony.

This story shows how easily abuse of freedom turned to death, murder and the destruction of society on this island. Pitcairn depicts on a small scale what happens in the world at large when freedom becomes a tool used to dominate and damage others. It shows the fall of man in straightforward and graphic terms. It is a picture of Genesis chapter 3. In it there are no grounds for blaming God or anyone else. It shows humanity gone wrong through its own deliberate fault. On a small scale the Pitcairn saga illustrates the mess in the world caused by man. All was not lost. The solution came from outside. It seemed impossible for the community to redeem itself. The Bible was found and through its message the community was transformed.

Similar stories of community transformation have been reported in more recent times. Another interesting example was seen when the American forces visited the Japanese island called Okinawa during World War Two, as reported by war correspondent, Clarence Hall. The island was in a very sad condition and the inhabitants were without hope or direction. But the forces found one village called Shimmabuke which was totally different. Its streets and homes were spotlessly clean. Its citizens were friendly and polite. Why was this village so different from the others? Thirty years before, a missionary stopped at Shimmabuke on his way to Japan. He won two men to Christ, Shosei Kina and his brother Mojon, and gave them a Bible. Through them the entire village became Christian and village life was transformed.

One of the greatest transformations has been seen in the land of Uganda. Uganda used to be known as the land of witchcraft. In the 1960s there were years of catastrophe with the rise of communist governments. Then in 1975 Idi Amin took over and declared the country to be an Islamic state, even though only three per cent of the population was Muslim. A large percentage of the population was killed and the economy was devastated. The situation failed to improve with his successor, Obote. In the midst of the great trials and difficulties, people began to really pray as they had never prayed before. One Christian leader, John Mulinde, reports that at this time 10,000 Christians began to meet in secret and 80 per cent committed themselves to pray day and night until God moved to help his people. Obote was deposed in 1986. Then came AIDS which rapidly became devastating and widespread. Uganda had the highest rate of HIV infection in the world.

It was estimated that by 1997, one third would be dead and one third would be unable to walk. But the Christians prayed and fasted with a powerful intensity. The situation was turned around totally. The AIDS rate began to decline rapidly. In 1998 President Museveni said, "In him (Christ), I find the inner strength, principles and lifestyle that can help me, and all Uganda's peoples, to solve our individual and national problems ... He is regarded as the greatest authority on human relationships ever to have lived."

In 2000, during the millennial celebrations, the First Lady publicly handed the country back to God for the next 1,000 years. Transformation was brought about because ordinary Ugandans began to take seriously the call of God to pray for their nation.

These stories show the impact people have made in society, through believing prayer and the words of the Bible. By working and praying together, whole cities and even countries can be transformed. This process is set in motion when we pray, but it is never easy. The sacrifices made by Christians in Uganda were extreme but as a result God moved in power. The Christians were often praying through long nights of darkness before the dawn broke. As Basilea Schlink, founder of a Lutheran community said, "If the glory of God is to break into your service you must go out into the night."

One of the tragedies of our comfortable existence in Western Christianity is that the call to go into the night and take up the cross and follow Christ is not heard clearly. We are encouraged to come to Christ for peace and forgiveness and reconciliation. All of these are important. But there is still the call of Christ. (Mark 8:34) "If any man would come after me let him deny himself and take up his cross and follow me." This means going out into the night where the problems are. We cannot do this alone but together we can build towards community transformation.

Does Prayer Really Change Things?

I learnt in a practical way the love of God when our family lived in Cyprus for six years from 1990 to 1996. I was invited to lead a church in Limassol in 1990. But whilst in Limassol our faith was tested. We had moved out to Cyprus as a family of seven, but did not always know where the finances were coming from. Once we completely ran out of food. I was shopping at that time, and recall going to a shop and looking at the price of vegetables. It was just before the celebration of the Greek Easter when all the vegetables increased in price as the Cypriots stopped eating meat. I had planned to make cauliflower cheese for my children but the price of cauliflowers had soared beyond what we could afford. I prayed to the Lord in the shop. I knew he was my heavenly Father and he could not abandon us. Empty-handed I returned home and opened the kitchen door. There in front of me on the table were three gigantic cauliflowers in addition to lots of other vegetables.

God had not neglected us. He was still our Father. He cared for us. He loved to provide for us. Two weeks later, without mentioning our needs to anyone, huge bags full of meat arrived outside our front door on three separate days. On the third occasion I ran to the door and saw someone running away quickly. It was a man who owned a small shop. I had spent a lot of time talking with him but I had not mentioned my needs to him. But God saw and he knew. God inspired him to come and help us in our need. God was truly our Father and was responsive to the needs of our family, his children.

God is a God of relationship. He loves to hear and answer the cries of his children. He loves to transform our circumstances when we reach out to him in faith. God not only wants to meet us in our need, he wants to use us to bring transformation into society. As we pray and advance together, who knows what God will do with us? This process is by no means automatic, though. We see, in Christ, that God became incarnate in human form. God came and lived among us as a living person. Wherever Christ went, the sick came to him from every place and were healed. The lame, the blind and the lepers – all came to him. At his touch or by his voice they were healed. Wherever Christ went, change and wholeness followed.

Similarly he sent out his disciples on two occasions, first the twelve, and later seventy. (Luke 9 and 10) As the twelve went out, Christ told them to preach the Kingdom of God, to heal, to cure diseases and to take authority over demons. (Luke 9:1-2) As these disciples moved out, community transformation began to happen. They would be received into houses where they would sit down and eat meals with families.

The first step was to establish relationships with the people of those villages. As they stayed and talked with the villagers, there would be openings to share the message of Jesus and the Kingdom that he was bringing in. They would, no doubt, describe some of the wonderful things they had seen Jesus do and would pass on some of his teaching. As they talked, the hearts of the listeners would begin to rise in hope. The sick would then be brought in and they would be touched and healed. The blind would see and the lame would walk. The disciples would cast out the demons. The Kingdom of God had come into those places visited by the disciples. Already there were the beginnings of community transformation.

Before Christ left the earth he passed over his authority to the twelve apostles in these words; "All authority has been given to me in heaven and on earth. Go therefore and make disciples of all the nations ...

and lo, I am with you always, even to the end of the age." (Matthew 28:18-20) He was saying, "Where you go, I go. What you do, I do." And so his kingdom came in. Before he left he promised them the Holy Spirit. He then breathed upon them as a sign that they would receive the Holy Spirit in power shortly after his death and resurrection. (John 20:22)

As the early community gathered together, they spent most of the time praying and seeking the presence and power of God. They did everything together. As they prayed, the power of God came upon them. They were filled with the Holy Spirit and moved out into Jerusalem, Judaea and Samaria. The Holy Spirit came on Paul and he preached the good news in the centre of the Roman Empire within a generation.

What is happening here is this; where Paul and the disciples go, transformation occurs. Transformation does not happen by chance. God is not sending bolts out of the blue to situations far distant from Jerusalem. Rather he uses his apostles and his followers to take the gospel into situations where it had not been before. As the good news penetrates these situations, so there is community transformation.

It is important to appreciate that this process involves us working in co-operation with God. We sometimes expect God to answer prayer whilst he is waiting for us to act. Prayer can then become an abdication of our responsibility. God seeks to work together with us, and wishes to use us to forward his kingdom and purposes.

It was when the disciples touched people that they were healed. It was as Peter was out walking, that his shadow fell on people and they were healed. It was where the disciples went and walked that transformation occurred. There seems to be a mistaken belief, prevalent in Western Christianity, that somehow expects God to do everything – particularly those things that we would prefer not to do ourselves! He is usually telling us to get on and do those things that he wants us to do. The Holy Spirit is given to those who ask so that we might then become the people of God on earth.

God creates and then moves in power by his Holy Spirit. As we go and work in his name, things will happen and lives will be changed. We are the transforming power of God. As we move together in love, unity and prayer so transformation will follow in our train. That is why, in our generation, it is so important to see the church moving together in power. The time has passed for us to remain in tiny churches and denominations. We need to work in large groups and express in the cities and countries of this world our unity and togetherness.

Transformation was brought about in Cali, Colombia as thousands gathered for all night prayer meetings in a soccer stadium. Drug cartels were overthrown and brought to justice. This has been vividly portrayed in a series of documentaries called "Transformations." The same happened in Uganda where massive meetings for prayer were held. This hunger for transformation of our society needs to grip us at a deep level. The day of small things is over. We must come together in large groups to pray and God will pour out his Spirit, to move in power among us.

There is a sense in which all of this is conditional. God does not force his way upon us. Revival is not the result of an action by an omnipotent God who chooses to send revival in one spot, and decides not to send it in another. Rather God, as the parent and the lover of his creation, is responsive to us. God is a Father to us and responds like a father to our requests. The Bible is also full of the relationship between Jesus and the Father. These verses show this unique relationship. "Truly, truly, I say to you, the Son can do nothing of himself, unless it is something he sees the Father doing; for whatever the Father does, these things the Son also does in like manner." (John 5:19) The picture we have of Christ is one of constant communion with God, his Father. From that divine communion and vital communication sprang the divine action plan which Jesus enacted. As Christ demonstrated a life of prayer with his Father, the disciples were entranced. They saw that relationship and said, "Lord, teach us to pray."(Luke 11:1)

Jesus then spent time teaching them how to pray. Our aim must be to share God's heart and to pray together. As we hear what he is saying so we are inspired to do things in his name and the Kingdom of God grows and grows. This is not an individual thing but it is collective. As we come together before God and ask him, so he pours out his power and his divine commission upon us.

There are many passages in the Bible, which show that God is responsive to us. One of these is the story of when Jeremiah visits the house of the potter. Jeremiah 18:1 starts like this, "The word which came to Jeremiah from the Lord saying, 'Arise and go down to the potter's house and there I will announce my words to you.' Then I went down to the potter's house and there he was making something on the wheel. But the vessel he was making of clay was spoiled in the hand of the potter; so he remade it into another vessel, as it pleased the potter to make.

"Then the word of the Lord came to me saying, 'Can I not, O house of Israel, deal with you as this potter does?' declares the Lord. 'Behold like the clay in the potter's hand so are you in my hand, O house of Israel. At one moment I might speak concerning a nation or concerning a kingdom to uproot, pull down or to destroy it; if that nation against which I have spoken turns from its evil I will relent concerning the calamity I planned to bring on it. Or at another moment I might speak concerning a nation or concerning a kingdom to build up or to plant it; if it does evil in my sight by not obeying my voice then I will think better of the good with which I had promised to bless it.'"

It seems that nothing could be clearer than this. God is listening to the prayers of his people and is acting according to how the people respond to him. God wants to hear from us. God is saying to an evil nation that if it turns from its wicked way then he will hear and will forgive. He will turn again, and he will build and plant them. But if they will not hear his voice then their sin will lead them into destruction. God is offering the nation an option at a critical point in their history. Destruction did not need to happen and there was a way of preventing it. The sad tale was that the nation in Jeremiah's time chose to continue in rebellion against God and was forced to go into captivity. Much of the nation was destroyed. However from the captivity a small number would return who would rebuild and focus once again, for a limited time, on God's plans.

God deals with us in the same way today. He is not sitting in heaven, deciding to send revival to one place and not to another or to send healing to one person and not to another. Rather he is waiting for those of us who belong to him and who love him to come together to seek his face and to call out to him, so that he may then come and bless us. John Wesley said, "God does nothing but in answer to believing prayer."

In our emphasis on God being all-powerful, all-knowing, and infinite, we have often lost the sense that God is actually our spouse, our lover, our friend, and he is waiting to hear from us. God wishes to be close to us. Jesus is emphasizing constantly that God is our Father. The difficulty with an over emphasis on the infinite qualities of God is that sometimes this can cause him to seem far away, whilst Jesus has come to reveal him to us as near and present. Hebrews 12:22 makes this point. We have not come to a mountain filled with smoke and terrifying in aspect, but rather "we have come to Mount Zion and to the city of the living God, the heavenly Jerusalem and to myriads of angels."

Instead of there being all that smoke and fire causing terror to the hearts of the Israelites as they looked at the burning, smoking mountain, by contrast we have come into a living vibrant community and into loving relationship. He is the great lover of our souls. This is why he waits to hear from us and when we speak to him, he is delighted. He loves to hear and answer our requests.

CHAPTER 8

CAN I BE FREE FROM THE PAIN INSIDE?

—ʍ—

A strange thing once happened on the American railways. A very long freight train had been travelling non-stop 25 miles during the night in 1898. On arrival at its destination they were amazed to discover that the refrigerator car had totally disappeared. This seemed impossible. How could it have become detached from the train? Three weeks later the mystery was solved when the refrigerator car was found damaged at the foot of an embankment surrounded by trees. This is what had happened. While rounding a sharp steep curve, the car became uncoupled at both ends and then toppled from the rails on the steep bend. The rear section of the train then caught up with, and coupled itself again to the front. This is another example of the amazing-but-true series!

So far in this book we have been looking at the mess the world is in and how we can understand God to be a God of love in the midst of the very obvious trauma and pain. We have taken a look at the image of God, which he has planted in us, and how we need to be free so that we can serve God in this world. We have considered examples of how the church can make a difference, despite the dreadful hurt and distress all around us. We considered the problem of suffering and how best we could understand it from a biblical perspective. "All of this may be interesting," you say, "but what about little old me?" Is there any help for the victim? Can we offer any help to the victims of rape, sexual abuse, and other major traumas that people have sustained?

Let us return to the illustration of the disappearing railway carriage. It had completely disappeared from view and could not easily be traced. When it was found it was badly damaged. This has parallels to our own lives. There are things in the "train" of our lives which have become derailed and detached and may remain hidden from view. Past pain and hurt often cause damage, which may remain hidden. The memories of these hurts and traumas may be sequestered so that the individual may not even realize that they are still there. Getting to the source of these hurts and wounds is usually the first step on the path of healing. It is the things that are hidden away that will do us damage. There is a tendency to try to push painful memories under the carpet. This is futile. They will come out and will damage our lives in the future. Like the refrigerator car, they have to be found so they can be mended. We may not necessarily remember the sources of pain in our lives as often they will be buried in childhood. Accessing these causes of pain is the first step in finding resolution.

Sometimes we have mistakenly thought that it is important to try to bury the past. In Philippians 3:13-14 Paul states, "Brethren, I do not regard myself as having laid hold of it yet; but one thing I do, forgetting what lies behind and reaching forward to what lies ahead, I press on toward the goal for the prize of the upward call of God in Christ Jesus." Many will have heard this verse taught in such a way as to imply that we should forget about the past and concentrate on the future. We may have been encouraged to believe that the past is all sorted out and we do not need to bother ourselves about it any longer. We are told, "Listen to Paul when he says 'Forgetting what lies behind.'"

This is another place where the context is extremely important. Paul is saying that his previous credentials and accomplishments in terms of his birth-right, his abilities, his training as one of the group called the Pharisees and his righteous former life are of no value to him now. None of these things are any good in gaining him standing before God. Previously he had thought that they might earn him some acceptance before God. Now he has learnt a new and fundamental truth. It is only by the grace of Jesus Christ that we find entry into the presence of God through faith in Christ. That is why he says that the former things, those things he had once relied on to get him a place before God, are now useless. He must depend totally on the grace and the love of Christ and forget these useless credentials from his past.

This verse has nothing to do with previous problems and difficulties we may have faced. They will surface in different ways in our lives unless they are resolved. It is no good to try to pretend that everything is all right and that some things never happened. All that will do is cement the problems more deeply into us. We have to get the past weeds rooted out of our lives.

As a boy I helped my mother weed the garden, albeit reluctantly. She would always emphasize the importance of getting the roots out. I would struggle with the deep-rooted docks and stinging nettles. Unless the roots came out my mother was not fully satisfied. She knew the weeds would grow again. The same is true of our lives. Problems are often deep rooted in us. These problems need to be identified at their source before they can be effectively dealt with.

I believe this is why Christians in the public eye need to be rigorous not only with their current behaviour, but also in sorting out the past. Otherwise they can end up, still unsorted, in major positions of leadership and public view. With the responsibility comes stress and pressure, and with the added stress the unsorted past problems tend to emerge. The leader might then try to bury the problem, believing that this problem could not possibly be happening to him or her now in his or her current position of leadership. There can easily arise a position of unreality in which the struggles of the leader are pushed down rather than brought to the surface. To whom can the Christian leader turn for help? If the leader cannot find help, then his life and ministry may be irreparably damaged. Not only may the Christian leader's life and ministry be ruined but also those who have followed may be damaged and hurt. Depending on the extent and public profile of the ministry, the entire world may get to know and the Christian faith brought into disrepute. Getting past problems properly sorted out might be extremely important for some Christian leaders.

It is vital for Christian leaders to be surrounded by loving, prayerful and accountable friends who will not only encourage but will also rebuke if necessary before it is too late. In the church there is a great need for accountability for all of us. There is a mistaken assumption that when we become Christians all past problems automatically disappear and no longer need attention. This is not the case. It is unusual to find the person who has not in some way been damaged in his or her childhood or at school. We carry the wounds of the past. The experiences of childhood mould our beings and help form our personalities. Where those experiences have been traumatic, the adult will carry the record of that trauma unless it is resolved.

It is important to try and understand past problems, and then find help for them. In this process two things are necessary. The first is to have good theology. Simply, this is to believe that Christ wants to bring healing and strength into our hurt and pain. He is full of love for everyone in need. He has the power to meet us in our problems. He wants to do this through the ministry of his servants. Secondly, it is important to have good psychology, so we know where the problems are likely to lie and how to deal with them. Good theology and good psychology belong together. As Scott Peck, a psychiatrist, has said, "Good theology makes good psychology."

If we are able to get our psychology and theology together when facing people's problems, we will be able to offer appropriate help that will alleviate some of the difficulties. By God's grace we will become more accurate in our ministry to others. We will be able to hit the mark. (Although the Lord may give us direct light on our past difficulties, it is best not to dig around oneself, unless a trained counsellor or minister is guiding this process.)

In Greek mythology, many suitors were annoying Penelope after Ulysses had been away for ten years. Penelope was expected to remain faithful, whatever the antics of Ulysses! Imagining him to be dead, she at last promised to marry the one who could shoot through twelve rings with an arrow that Ulysses had used in the past. As preparations were coming together for this unusual contest, Ulysses arrived disguised as a beggar. One by one the various suitors came forward but found they were unable even to bend the bow. Then Ulysses said, "Beggar as I am, I was once a soldier and there's still some strength in these old limbs of mine. Let me try." The suitors laughed at him but Penelope, perhaps with womanly intuition, insisted that he should be allowed to try. With ease he bent the bow, and the arrow went sailing through the rings. It was Ulysses. Penelope threw herself into his arms.

With the light of Christ to lead and guide us and with understanding of the human condition we, like Ulysses, will be able to hit the target and get the problems sorted out that may otherwise remain unresolved. Christ will help us bend the bow and send the arrow to its mark. We will find ourselves able to shoot really straight and see people's lives transformed as we bring together the disciplines of psychology, psychiatry and the Christian faith.

So Where Does Depression Come From?

Adoniram Judson, missionary to Burma, became the father of the American missionary movement. He was in Burma for several years before he saw any conversions. He worked extremely hard to establish Christianity in this place and many of his children died there. He was imprisoned in appalling circumstances. During a time of very hard work his wife died. He was not with her at this time and he felt extremely guilty about this. He was unable to forgive himself for not being with his wife but instead of allowing himself to grieve, he plunged himself into further work. He imagined that he could overcome his grief in this way. He was seeking to assuage the pain of his loss and false guilt by burying himself in activity. This does not work. It only serves to make the difficulties worse. Problems, which are submerged or buried, become more difficult to deal with and more damaging. They will emerge in new ways that usually cause more pain and hurt. In Judson's case this is what happened.

After some time his work output slowed and he then withdrew from social company. He went out into the jungle and cut a shallow grave in the ground. He then spent days by the side of the grave in absolute and total despair. Because he sought to bury the problem rather than deal with it, the problem increased tenfold. His plight was known to his fellow Christians who poured out their hearts in love and concern for their stricken leader. Slowly, through the love and counsel of fellow Christians, he was able to emerge from the slough of despond. In the end he came through. What he then experienced was that he had entered into a new phase in his ministry. Previously he had preached with little effect. Now crowds came to see and hear him and many became Christians. He was able to preach widely across Burma and see many people come to know Christ.

Getting to the origin or root of a problem is vitally important. When recently I was trying to find my way through a difficult problem in human relationships, it proved important to investigate the origin of the problem. When I was able to identify the origin, I could see much more clearly how to deal with the current situation. The same is true about problems that we may have in our lives. Understanding the origins will help us find the solutions.

Depression is a disorder in which many different factors may combine together to lead to someone becoming unwell. I want to look briefly at depression since it causes so much suffering. I will then move on to consider in outline the help that may be available. This is not intended to be a medical or comprehensive account but more a way of illustrating the different factors that may be involved.

As a psychiatrist working with the elderly, I meet many patients who are depressed. There may be contributory factors dating back to early life. Some patients have suffered the loss in early life of parents either through death, separation or divorce. Others may have suffered physical or sexual abuse and have carried scars from these through their lives. For others, parents may simply have failed in their parenting by being absent or otherwise unavailable for all kinds of reasons. Some families suffer much more from depression than others and genetic factors are believed to be involved.

Between individuals there is marked variation in temperament. Some tend to be more withdrawn and find social contact more difficult. They form friends less easily and have less good support mechanisms. In general they tend to have a negative view of life. They may carry through life the tendency to feel guilty and blame themselves when things go wrong. Self-doubt may blight their lives and make it much more difficult for them to make purposeful decisions. Many may overcome these difficulties. For others they may remain and lead to anxious or depressive personality traits.

Some may display longstanding abnormal patterns of behaviour or problems with dependency on drugs or alcohol, which may result in alienation from friends and family. Thus the elderly person is isolated from the usual support and help available in old age. In some cases the children may have abandoned their parents, or remaining family may have died or been killed in war or may be absent by living abroad. Some or all of these factors can make the entry into the later years of life a lonely and depressing time. These individuals will be more prone to depressive illness.

Although these considerations are often in the background, it is usually more recent events that have plunged the person into depression. This may be the result of the loss of a spouse, close friend or relative. Often elderly persons have had to cope with two or three significant losses in short periods of time. Changes in living arrangements such as having to move into a care home can have a profound effect and most find the loss of autonomy very difficult. For others it can actually be devastating. In some it is the loss of role that is important. A person may have had a very satisfying role as a father, mother, or wage earner and provider and suddenly that is taken away. The children leave the nest, retirement takes place, and it may prove a struggle to fill the day easily. Physical illness often makes things worse and may lead to a loss of abilities. Ongoing, chronic physical illness can be extremely difficult to cope with. At other times loss of memory and early cognitive decline compound the situation.

When depression is severe it is unwise to try to root out the causes. What I mean by severe depression is otherwise referred to as depressive illness. Here the mood is persistently low. The person has usually lost most of their interests and is unable to enjoy anything. Sleep and appetite are affected, as is the ability to concentrate. There may be marked weight loss. The person finds it difficult to carry on with their usual activities, and may be plagued with feelings of guilt and self-blame. Reactions may be slowed down and the speed of thought reduced.

Some may become agitated. Life will be an effort and may seem at times not worth living. Suicidal thoughts may emerge. Recognition of this condition is important, as the person will need expert help. The person is too fragile to cope with understanding the reasons why he or she might be depressed. This is not the time to dig around for causes with the person. At this stage rest, removal from responsibility and medical care will be necessary. As improvement takes place, the patients themselves will often want to look for the underlying causes.

There may be deep-rooted problems that have been there from childhood or early life. Often it is people who know the patient best who will have insight into these problems. Frequently it is helpful for family, psychiatrists, and Christian ministers to work together in seeking to heal and bring restoration into people's lives.

People cope with problems in different ways. Some people seem to have the strength to cope with illness and difficulties without too much trouble, whilst others seem to go under in similar situations. The way in which we respond to current crises and difficulties is often rooted in the past. When faced with difficulties in the present, our emotional memory kicks into gear as it remembers similar situations from the past. Depending on the nature of those past experiences one situation may fill one person with dread, whilst the same situation may seem utterly trivial to another. All forms of illness may be made much worse by the coping mechanisms which we use to deal with them. For example, some may seek escape from depression by abuse of alcohol, which can intensify low mood.

This is a poem written by a young mother, and ex-patient of a colleague, who has struggled to break free from alcohol abuse. (Printed with permission)

Why do I drink? I wish I knew,
Binges and so much came out of the blue.
I am in rehab, my children in care,
I need out of this mess; it is too hard to bear.
Then everything seems good again,
I forget my faults and all the pain.
That's what I have to understand,
I cannot have a drink in my hand.
I need to be a sober mum or not at all,
Music loud, me drunk, I cannot hear their call.
I always tried to fool myself and only drank
    at night,
What I never realized, my children woke in
    fright.
A bottle gets me drunk and that's as far as
    it goes,
My children bring me happiness that really
    grows and grows.
The answer is there. I cannot have my cake
    and eat it,
So with everything, and all it takes I have to
    really beat it.

She wrote this other poem:

"What is wrong mummy?" Why am I here?
How can I say it is to do with my beer?
She is only four; it is hard to explain,
I tell her I am sick, she will be home soon
    again.
She said, "Okay mummy" then turns to play,
I wonder what she is thinking in her wee
    head today.
I sense they are happy, but fear they are not,
Worry and pain going through me a lot.
I pray the day will come where we can share
    tomorrow,
To be able to break away from all this
    sorrow.

The pain is very obvious. A young mother is trapped in the problems of alcohol abuse, and risks losing her children as a result.

Christians can find it difficult to cope with depression because they may be told that they should not be depressed. This can be the message from ministers and well-meaning friends. The truth is that many of those who have followed God closely have suffered from depression. In an ideal world depression would not exist. But we do not live in an ideal world. We live in a broken and messed-up world. Christians suffer from depression as well as others. King David was one of the men in the Bible described as being "after God's own heart." (Acts 13:22) Many of his Psalms describe his personal experience. In some of them we see right into David's heart. For this reason, right down the ages all kinds of people have found that the Psalms speak directly into their own situations.

In some of these psalms, it is pretty clear that David became very, very depressed. Take these verses from Psalm 6:6-7; "I am weary with my sighing; every night I make my bed swim; I dissolve my couch with my tears. My eye has wasted away with grief; it has become old because of all my adversaries." He does not exactly seem full of the joy of the Lord! From this Psalm and other similar psalms, it is evident that David has classic features of a depressive illness. He is awake at night; he is losing weight; he is crying; he is not eating; he cannot concentrate, and at times he even asked the Lord to take away his life.

Christian history is full of those who have been through similar trials. Hudson Taylor, a well-known missionary, suffered deep bouts of depression as did Spurgeon, the famous preacher. As Christians face depression, it is important to realize that we are not alone. In general, although Christians may suffer from depression, religious belief does tend to protect against the effects of it. It has not always been easy to decide whether the protective element is due to the belief itself, or whether it is related to belonging to a group of like-minded people who are supportive. Probably it has to do with both. It is a privilege to know that Christ is with us and that we have eternal life. It gives a tremendous sense of purpose to life to know that we have the power of Christ to help us bring joy and gladness into the world. Certainly unbelievers have often been extremely unhappy.

Voltaire who prophesied the demise of Christianity wrote, "I wish I had never been born." Lord Byron who lived a life of pleasure wrote, "The worm, the canker, and grief are mine alone."

Sometimes we can give trite answers to those with depression. This is generally unhelpful. In 1800 a man entered the office of Dr James Hamilton in Manchester. The doctor was struck by his melancholy appearance and asked him about his problems. He replied that he was frightened of the world. He was depressed by life. He could find no happiness anywhere; nothing amused him. He had nothing to live for. He said, "If you can't help me, I shall kill myself." The doctor told him that he would not die. "You need to get out of yourself. You need a laugh; to get some pleasure from life." "What shall I do?" the melancholic man asked. The doctor told him to go to the circus to see Grimaldi the clown. He was the funniest man alive and Grimaldi would cure him. Pain crossed the sad man's face. He said simply: "Doctor, don't jest with me; I am Grimaldi!" Trite and simple answers do not help. This is not the way to help someone who is seriously depressed! Grimaldi was in need of proper care and attention.

Where Can I Find Help?

Elijah became suicidal and said, "It is enough; now O Lord, take my life, for I am not better than my fathers."(1 Kings 19:4) Elijah was one of the greatest prophets. He was the one whom the apostle Peter subsequently saw with Moses and Christ on the mountain of transfiguration. Yet here he wants to end his life. What can have led him to such low ebb? How has he become so overcome with self-blame as this verse indicates? The story is this. For over three years he had lived an isolated existence while King Ahab sought him everywhere to kill him. He had been blamed for the famine that was in the land. He thought he was the only true believer left.

After three years he challenged King Ahab, Queen Jezebel and 450 prophets of Baal to a showdown on Mount Carmel. It took all day long before the prophets of Baal gave up trying to bring fire from heaven. Then the fire of God fell following Elijah's prayer. The 450 prophets of Baal had to be rounded up and disposed of. Elijah then ran seventeen miles to Jezreel ahead of the king's chariot. He must have been absolutely wiped out, physically, mentally and emotionally. Then Jezebel threatened him with death and he was on the run again, but this time for his life. He then just totally collapsed, probably feeling terrible for running away and despaired of life. He probably did not suffer from true depressive illness but all the normal props of life to prevent depression had been blown away.

There are certain basic rules of happy existence. It is extremely important to maintain friendships and most relationships. (Some of course may be better not maintained!) We become much more vulnerable when isolated. Many people make basic mistakes by withdrawing from others when faced with relationship difficulties, rather than going through the process of honest reflection and forgiveness that may be necessary to bring healing. Others through their own dependency needs or failure to deal with anger end up thrusting others away. Shyness and inhibitions impede others from making satisfactory relationships. It is so sad to meet older people who literally have no relationships left to speak of. Relationships do have a tendency to be more difficult to form and sustain as we grow older. Often it is the ones made when we were younger that persist and remain most meaningful.

Secondly, occupation is important. There is nothing worse than the barrenness of doing nothing. We were not made to do nothing. Work is actually important. As we discussed in an earlier section, work is an expression of the image of God given to us. This work may not necessarily be work in the conventional sense. I am enjoying at present writing this book. This is not part of my normal work but it could be construed as work. It is certainly a satisfying occupation. Whether the results will merit the work put into it remains to be seen! Even if not, I personally feel enriched through writing it. Keeping in touch with interests and hobbies is important, particularly those that keep us socially interacting with others. God made us to be creative too and we need to find ways of expressing that creativity.

Frequently I suggest to my patients to take a sheet of paper at a time when they feel at their best (often, but not always, the evening) and write on it a plan for the following day. They should write down some things that would give them a sense of achievement and others that they would usually enjoy. The next day they are encouraged to follow the plan. Doing things is usually much better than doing nothing although in severe depression this may not be possible. The tasks need to be appropriate for the stage of illness that the person is in. Simple, achievable goals are much better than difficult ones which, if not completed, might leave a sense of frustration.

Maintaining a simple exercise programme is therapeutic mentally as well as physically. Looking to change overloaded schedules and imbalances in life is also important. Most people on their deathbeds will not say they wished they had spent more time in the office, though many might deeply regret spending too little time with their children. Having clearly worked out priorities in life helps in making sure that the urgent does not always crowd out the important. It is also important to meet our basic needs for food, sleep, clothing, shelter and safety. The depression of the prophet Elijah followed extreme exhaustion and depletion of basic requirements for living, as well as the enforced isolation he endured.

In helping the elderly, much is done to provide for their physical care. Less is done to provide for their emotional well-being. Understanding what gives each individual a sense of significance and importance is central to this. Part of this also involves encouraging people to maintain roles and responsibilities as far as possible.

These are all basics which help to maintain happy and fulfilled existence. Having a sense of worth and value is particularly important. This comes supremely from a correct relationship with God himself. We need to know God as Father and understand that we are forgiven and embraced by God himself. This gives us a purpose and value beyond ourselves and a hope of heaven.

If the depression becomes severe, medical help will be required. The person will need medication or physical forms of treatment. I have little hesitation in prescribing antidepressants to patients who are deeply depressed. They work well although response in the elderly is often a little slower than in the adult population. Other people may need help with anxiety or help in sleeping. In very serious depression, electro-convulsive treatment can be necessary. Patients who are suicidal in their depression, or failing to eat and drink, are often given this type of treatment, and usually it works very well.

Different forms of therapy can deal with varied problems in the person's life. Interpersonal therapy in the elderly can be very valuable. It can help the person to come to terms with relationship difficulties and he or she can then work out ways of working on these and be encouraged to reintegrate into societal groups, rather than withdrawing into isolation. Cognitive behaviour therapy is extremely valuable as a way of examining negative belief systems and then finding ways to overcome these.

Other forms of psychotherapy can help deal with deep, underlying emotional problems which may have been present from childhood. Sometimes the most important kind of therapy is just to be there and available to the person who is suffering. Supportive therapy in terms of listening, caring and loving is extremely important in helping people through the crisis of depression. Family, marital and group therapy may have their place. (I want to emphasise again that this section is drawing together some thoughts and ideas and is not meant to be a full and authoritative guide to this area.)

What About Past Problems?

When an employee of a bank in Idaho accidentally put a box of 8,000 cheques worth $850,000 on a table for rubbish, a nightmare occurred. The contents were shredded into quarter-inch pieces which were then dumped outside the bank. "I wanted to cry", said the bank supervisor. Most of the cheques had been cashed in the bank and were waiting transfer to the clearing-house. The loss would result in an accounting nightmare as most of them were still unrecorded. The bankers could not know who paid what to whom. They decided to reclaim the shredded pieces and painfully reconstruct each cheque. Fifty employees worked daily inside six rooms in an effort to reconstruct all those cheques. Our lives sometimes resemble all those shredded cheques. They are fragmented and in disorder. There appears to be no way to get them back into order. It seems like an impossible job to get things straightened out inside us.

Broadly speaking there are two categories of difficulty that people face. There are problems related mainly to current situations, and there are those that are related to past hurts and pain. People, in general, are less aware of the problems stemming from past experiences. The two groups of difficulties are related in that current problems may be related (but not always) to past traumas and adverse events. Problems related to current difficulties are easier to access, since these usually cause the person to seek help. The counsellor or minister will regard these as the presenting complaints. However, emotionally laden traumas and negative experiences perhaps from childhood may have been forgotten or covered over, either deliberately or sometimes subconsciously. In many cases the person may find the raw emotion of these past problems too difficult to face. Although often hidden away, these painful memories may erupt into consciousness when they are triggered by current events that are similar to the hurts experienced in the past. They may not fully emerge but often there may be the sense that something like this has happened before, and it was unpleasant. The current experience will be tainted by the past pain. It is for this reason that past unresolved hurts should not be ignored or buried. Rather in the right way and at the right time they should be allowed to emerge so they can be healed.

All Christians are called to serve each other by helping to carry the load of another. The apostle Paul says, "Bear one another's burdens and thereby fulfil the law of Christ."(Galatians 6:2) Every Christian in touch with the living Christ can bring a measure of support and help to those in distress. This is part of our common Christian calling to serve each other. So called "ministry" is just another word for service. Christ is the great healer and we are called to serve each other with his healing grace. Regarding Christ we read this, "He has sent me to bind up the broken-hearted, to proclaim liberty to captives and freedom to prisoners." (Isaiah 61:1) However experience and understanding of some of the ways in which the mind works can be very helpful. It is also important for all of us to recognize our limitations and to know when we need outside help.

A knowledge and understanding of types of secular therapy is valuable for the Christian involved in ministry. Some of these ways of seeking whole-ness are more useful in dealing with current problems and others are best employed in coming to grips with underlying deeper traumas stemming from past expe-riences. If the person receiving ministry is a Christian or sympathetic to the Christian faith, then inviting Christ by prayer to bring in his light and truth is, I believe, always beneficial. Jesus says, "I am the Light of the World; he who follows me will not walk in the darkness but will have the light of life." (John 8:12) Jesus can minister his truth and light into the dark places of the soul, bringing wholeness to the person.

Some forms of secular therapy are quite closely allied with Christian revelation and this should not be surprising. In the short section below I have not sought in any way to be exhaustive, but have concen-trated rather on one or two approaches that I have personally found valuable. Other Christians may find alternative methods work better for them. The main concern is not which particular way we may happen to prefer. The important thing is that those receiving ministry are healed and strengthened in their lives. As we minister in this way then Christ will be honoured and exalted.

The Lord's ways are very varied! I have worked alongside people who are acutely aware of what God is saying to an individual. Even without asking questions some are able, by special gifting from God, to go straight to the root of the problem and speak out a word that will bring healing. I thank God that he has given many such anointed ministers to his church. Other people may spontaneously, or following prayer, receive themselves a special word from the Lord. God works in various ways and through all kinds of people.

In Christian ministry, as in professional practice, I will seek first of all to establish whether or not any form of mental illness is present. If this is the case it will require quite a different approach. I will also seek to determine whether the individual has a Christian faith or is open to a Christian way of looking at the problems. If so, and with the person's permission, I will express openly my dependence on God and ask him, through prayer, to be involved in the ministry situation. Much will then depend on the kind of problem that the individual is facing. In some situations he or she may require the support of a listening ear through a difficult crisis.

At times the focus of ministry may be around current problems and difficulties which the person is experiencing. Clarification of these, using problem-solving techniques, will often be the first step towards the development of strategies that will lead to improvement or resolution of the difficulties. There may be major problems with relationships that will need to be explored and addressed. An understanding of the network of relationships in which the individual is involved, and the relative importance of each one to the individual may be valuable in guiding the way forward. Here, an understanding of the basic tenets of so-called Interpersonal Therapy can prove valuable. Repentance, forgiveness and restitution may all be needed as well, and Christ teaches us much about this area. (Matthew 18:15-35, 6:5-15 for example) At other times sinful thoughts or behaviour may need challenging.

Cognitive Behaviour Therapy is a very valuable skill. It shows the way our thoughts can affect our emotions and behaviour. If we have strongly negative thoughts then we may well feel low in mood, and in response, for example, withdraw from social events. Helping a person to examine his or her negative thoughts may be the first step towards recovery. We may make mistakes in our thinking by giving a negative flavour to everyday events. For example, if my secretary fails to greet me in the morning (which she never does!) I might start to think, "What have I done wrong?" and come up with all kinds of negative thoughts about the likely cause. If I believed these, without finding out the true cause my mood could begin to dip. I could begin to imagine, for example that my secretary did not like me or felt I was giving her too much work to do! The real explanation might lie in the last phone call she had taken. It may have nothing to do with me at all. Helping a person examine his or her thoughts and the ways these might affect mood and behaviour, and assisting in unravelling negative and incorrect thinking patterns can be vital. This approach fits well with biblical teaching. The apostle Paul teaches us, "And do not be conformed to this world, but be transformed by the renewing of your mind."(Romans 12:2) Again he advises, "Finally, brothers, whatever is true, whatever is noble, whatever is right, whatever is pure, whatever is lovely, whatever is admirable, if anything is excellent or praiseworthy, think about such things." (Philippians 4:8)

All the above, and many more approaches than I have mentioned, may be valuable in helping with current difficulties. My mentioning of the methods above is necessarily brief in the context of the overall theme of this book.

Often the problems lie at a deeper level. Despite dealing with current problems, the person is unable to shake off painful emotions which still are like a cloud over his or her life. Are there any ways of resolving these deeper problems? Here we find we are dealing with problems that may be long-standing and have often arisen in childhood. In other situations we may find ourselves needing to bring the power of Christ to confront demonic forces. This last area would need a book by itself!

I would like to share a few thoughts on a way which I have found valuable in helping with some of these deeper problem areas. Often the difficult emotions the person is experiencing are useful guides to the underlying problem, and I will spend some time clarifying these. I will pray asking Christ to help us find the roots of the painful emotions. I explain that the roots may lie in past, hurtful experiences.

For example in my own life, as a boy of nine I was moved from one class to a higher one when they realized I was performing better than they had expected. I was placed in a class where nobody talked to me for six months. Being rather shy and reticent by temperament did not make things any easier. Not only did I have to endure the silence and the lack of any friendship but I was also called names. One of the names which stuck was "Dopey." As I reflect on that time, I am able to see that the name had a negative impact on my self-worth and value. I also believed that I was very different from my class-mates and that I could not fit in. I had believed a lie about myself as a result of this damaging experience.

In many cases, painful memories hide behind current emotional problems. Along with the memory the individual will usually have believed a lie about him or herself from the past situation as a way of coming to terms with the pain involved. The lie is usually some kind of powerful negative statement about the self. This mistaken belief has often adversely affected the way the person thinks about him or herself from that time forward. These lies can be immensely powerful in moulding future thought patterns. In ministry, I find that the Lord reveals his truth to replace the lie as we ask him to do this. The ensuing peace which Christ brings is one of the hallmarks of true healing of the memory. This is much more powerful than my trying to tell the person the right answers.

Some time ago a lady came to see me who had been sexually abused by her grandfather. The abuse had happened on a regular basis for several years but she had been afraid to tell anyone about it. Now, as a married woman, she found intimate relations with her husband difficult as these triggered memories of the previous abuse she had suffered. She believed the lie that she was guilty and to blame in some way for what happened. Logical explanations that this was not the case failed to shift this underlying conviction. During ministry she experienced the calm assurance that the Lord had been present with her, holding her hand, even during the times that she had been abused. The Lord also spoke to her heart, telling her that she was not guilty and not to blame. She recently sent me a letter saying that although it had been emotionally difficult at the time, since then she has experienced a release from these memories of the past. She says that she continually holds on to what the Lord told her that day.

Working along these lines is not necessarily for everyone, but I find it helps people find freedom from their deep rooted pain. In the context of this book, I have only sketched in the broad details and am not giving the reader a model to copy. They illustrate some ways which I have found helpful. (Some of the above I have gleaned from Theophostic Ministry, the name having its origin in the Greek words for "God" and "light." Some of these insights are quite helpful in ministry. In particular the teaching on elucidating the lies associated with past memories is very valuable.)

The beautiful thing about Jesus is that he is able to undo the scars of the past much better and more effectively than any other counsellor. That is why the combination of psychological and psychiatric practice with Christian belief can be immensely powerful. My wife and I often work together in ministering in the way I have outlined. It is part of that "Philia" relationship of not only facing the same direction but also working together to bring healing into the lives of precious people.

CHAPTER 9

HOW CAN I MOVE ON FROM HERE?

———

Agostino d'Antonio, a sculptor from Florence, worked diligently but without success on a large piece of marble. "I can do nothing with it," he finally said. Other sculptors valiantly attempted to make something of the marble but gave up the difficult task. The stone lay discarded in the rubbish for 40 years. Walking about one day, Michelangelo espied the marble and recognized its potential. It was brought to his studio and he began to work on it. Ultimately his vision and work were successful. From that seemingly worthless stone was carved one of the world's masterpieces "David."

Christ himself was called the stone that the builders rejected. In dying, he became the chief cornerstone of a new building. Peter reminds us of this; "Behold I lay in Zion a choice stone, a precious corner stone and he who believes in him will not be disappointed." (1 Peter 2:6) Christ, rejected and outcast, has become the central piece of a whole new building. Peter goes on to say how important each one of us is. One of the chief aims of this book has been to show how special each of us is to God. Here again are Peter's words, "But you are a chosen race, a royal priesthood, a holy nation, a people for God's own possession, so that you may proclaim the excellencies of him who has called you out of darkness into his marvellous light."(1Peter 2:9)

God is used to taking the rubbish of the world and turning it into something beautiful for himself. It is only the Christian message that can effectively take a man from the gutter and transform him. This was the work of William Booth who delighted in seeing transformation at work in the redemption of lives from the gutter of late nineteenth century East London. Lives were transformed and lived to the full that otherwise would have been dead and buried.

The story of Humpty Dumpty is that he sat on the wall and had a great fall. Being so large and yet so fragile, the rhyme runs that "All the king's horses and all the king's men couldn't put Humpty together again." The power of Jesus, though, can mend lives shattered by the pain and suffering in life and bring restoration to every part. The great difficulty people have is accepting that they need help. If there were only the personal recognition that we cannot do everything ourselves and the willingness to look outside ourselves for help, then I am sure there would be a lot more people turning to Christ. Humility in God's eyes is very precious. I have aimed in this book to point a way for those who feel that their lives are shattered beyond repair like Humpty Dumpty's. Healing and help are available. Having the humility to reach out for God's help tends to cut across the general drift of life which encourages total self-sufficiency.

There are excellent reasons to reach out for help. Blaise Pascal, a seventeenth century mathematician, physicist and theologian wrote, "Let us weigh the gain and the loss, in wagering that God is. Consider these alternatives: If you win, you win all. If you lose you lose nothing. Do not hesitate, then, to wager that he is." There is irrefutable logic in Pascal's argument.

God never seems terribly bothered about exactly why we turn to him. Some may do it because it seems the best option available. C S Lewis, the famous author, followed Christ at first most reluctantly, because it seemed there was no other rational alternative. Others may follow initially because it is the only hope left to them in the gutter of life. Somehow I don't think God minds. He is well able to pick up the pieces and sort us out.

I can still go to the street corner where God spoke into my heart and simply said, "I love you and accept you just the way you are." Before that I had been in turmoil inside. I could not believe that God would accept me and love me. Can I explain how God spoke to my heart? No, it is beyond me. It was certainly not an audible voice. But it was extremely clear nonetheless, and proved life-transforming. I knew from that moment forward that I was different, and the doubts, which I had faced now had a solution.

Ever since that time I have been free, through the word that God spoke into my heart to liberate me from the lies of my childhood. Unfortunately, as a child I had been taken to many services where hell-fire had been preached at me. That had made me terribly afraid and uncertain, although fear may well have prevented me from going astray completely! But it is not healthy to live in fear. Jesus Christ, through this living word, brought me into a much more joyful walk with God.

Another aim in writing this short book has been to examine the character of God as revealed in the simple statement "God is love." I have sought to show that love is the chief attribute of God. I have looked briefly at the way in which that love is revealed to the world.

This book has tried to analyze some of the problems of suffering and pain. Suffering is a universal problem. I believe failure to understand its origin has caused damage to our lives. As Raymond Lull, a missionary martyred in the fourteenth century said, "The more you understand, the better you can believe." I believe that logic and reason are part of the image that God has given us. I have wanted to apply reason and logic to the problem of suffering. I have suggested that suffering is due to the continuance in the world of Satan who is the "ruler of this world."

Light, of course, cannot dwell with darkness. A group of people went into one of the deepest caves under the earth. The darkness was pitch-black. It was impossible to see a hand in front of one's face. For emotional support people held hands tightly in the deep cave. The guide then lit a single match and the place was filled with light. In the same way Satan and his followers bring darkness and pain and suffering into the world, but a single light can be part of the process of overcoming the darkness. We are never to be afraid of Satan and his forces, but rather to believe that through the power of Christ we are more than able to conquer them.

I want this book to be a message of love and hope to those who are hurting. For this reason I have sought to emphasize the love of God. God is the great lover of our souls. We see his Agape love in his sacrifice on the cross. We are amazed that he wants us to be his friends. "But I have called you friends, for all things that I have heard from my Father I have made known to you". (John 15:15)

He has called us into a love relationship with himself. It is he who calls us his friends and his brothers and brings us into the family of his love. As we share the love in the heart of God, so we are able to radiate that love through our lives. It is my prayer that this book may prove the beginning of a process of finding healing for some. The problems of our lives often follow childhood experiences. There are some pointers in this book, which may help people to find ways out of their hurt and pain through experiencing the presence and power of Christ. This will usually be through the loving and wise ministry of others.

Seeing A New Horizon

In the stormy North Sea, near the coast of the Netherlands, there lay a ledge of rocks where there had been many shipwrecks. Pirates, who inhabited the islands, would loot the vessels and murder the stranded ship's crews. Finally, the Netherlands government decided once for all to rid the island of pirates. They asked a young Dutch lawyer to carry out the task. It was a grim, barren place. The lawyer bravely decided to live on the island as he determined to make the island beautiful. People told him that trees or plants would never live but would be destroyed by the violent storms. He refused to be discouraged. He planted trees – 100 the first year, and then more every year for the 50 years he lived there. As the trees grew, the island became a bird sanctuary. A pair of storm-driven nightingales took refuge on the island and the island later became host to a colony of nightingales. The fame of "The Island of Nightingales" spread far and wide.

God loves to bring order out of chaos and beauty from barrenness. Sharing the resurrection life of Christ is all about this. As we offer our lives to him, so he fills us with his Spirit. We can bring beauty into the world like the Dutch lawyer did on the island. As we are set free from the chains of our past, and the impediments caused by the wounds of past experiences and their associated lies, we become able to share more completely in the life of the resurrected Christ. French priest John Baptiste Marie Vianney said, "It is always springtime in the heart that loves God."

Celebrating continual Easter as reality in our lives brings springtime to our hearts, and sets us free from the chains that bind us. Easter not only is a celebration of the resurrection of Jesus Christ but also is a celebration of a whole new order. Christ is raised from the dead to begin a whole new world movement. He calls us to bring the good news to all nations, and to bring regeneration and life into every area. There is to be life in the arts, life in music, life in science, life in politics, and life in every area of human endeavour. He calls us to bring in a whole new order. God wants constantly to bring order out of chaos. Even ecology will be affected.

God calls us to bring beauty and order from the barrenness of our environment. The command in the garden given to man to look after creation and to name the animals, has never been superseded. As Christians, part of our calling is to take responsibility for our environment and not to pollute it. Man still holds a unique position as governor of the world that God made. Through man the whole creation is to be brought into harmony. In this resurrection order we are called to bring life and light to the world.

At times I have reflected on what it may mean to have new bodies like the body of Christ. We are promised that one day we will have new resurrection bodies. It is interesting to note that in the post-resurrection experiences of Christ, he is able to travel from one point to another point instantaneously. He is also able to pass through closed doors. He eats bread and fish with the disciples This is no hallucination. This is a living person. He invites them to touch him and put their hands in the prints of the nails. The disciples are so transformed by their experience of the living Christ that they preach the word of God without any shadow of fear and if tradition holds true, each one of them was martyred for his faith.

What is interesting though, is to reflect on the possibilities that the new body might give us. I never cease to be amazed at the vastness of the universe. Light is only now reaching us from stars 13 billion light years away! This gives great antiquity to the universe. Personally I cannot accept any argument that would say that light is created in mid-course and then somehow reaches us, being only a few thousand years old. No, the world and the universe are of great antiquity. But within this antiquity and vastness, what potential there is for the future! Who knows whether we will be able to move with our resurrection bodies from one part of the universe to another instantaneously?

If the image of God in us is an image that brings order out of chaos, we can continue to work with joy and ability and have the whole universe as our stage. Indeed, the created universe which has never been explored and is unlikely ever to be, will become a vast theatre of God's presence. We may be able to work out God's command in every corner of the universe. It is impossible to see the vast universe being wasted and thrown on some cosmic scrap heap. God does not create, then to waste. Our future lives will be filled with joyful creativity. C S Lewis has said, "Joy is the serious different business of heaven." I cannot imagine that we will be sitting around playing harps.

Yes, we will be worshipping, but we will have the vast universe as our scene of operations.

There will be judgment on Satan and all those under his sway. The victory Christ won on the cross will be fully and finally acted out. The fire of judgment will fall. This fire will purify the current created order. (2 Peter 3:10) Following this cleansing from evil the universe will be set free from its bondage to decay and we will be changed. Paul writes, "The creation itself also will be set free from its slavery to corruption into the freedom of the glory of the children of God."(Romans 8:21)

First, those who are children of God are set free from the everlasting cycle of decay and sin and death, and then the universe follows the transformation of the children of God and becomes gloriously free. Earthquakes and so-called natural disasters, reflective of a world in which sin is unchecked and Satan is active, will have no place in the new order. The children of God will continue that enduring relationship begun on earth in faith but now continuing by sight, as they see the everlasting creator whose name is love. This everlasting life is not all future. We have already tasted our inheritance and it tastes good.

Catching The Wind

A remarkable story is told about a costly ruby that for a long time was considered of no real value. Gustaf Gillman was at work in his shop when a labourer called John Mihok walked in and handed him a rough, red stone. "I want you to cut and polish this," he said. Gustaf Gillman's eyes almost popped out of his head. He was very curious as to its origin and asked Mihok about it. "My father picked it up in Hungary 50 years ago," Mihok replied. "He thought it was a pretty pebble. When I landed in this country, I found it in my pack. It has been lying around the house ever since. The children played with it. My last baby cut his teeth on it. One night I dreamed it was a diamond worth a lot of money, but it is not a diamond. It is red."

Gillman told him that it was a pigeon-blood ruby. "What might it be worth?" Mihok asked. "I would say anywhere from 100 to 250 thousand dollars," said Gillman. Mihok leaned heavily against the door for support. The big red stone has since been cut and is one of the largest and finest rubies in the world.

It is not difficult to neglect the most precious things in the world. Many do this with the Kingdom of God. Jesus tells us that the Kingdom of heaven is like costly treasure. (Matthew 13:44) "The kingdom of heaven is like a treasure hidden in the field, which a man found and hid again; and from joy over it, he goes and sells all that he has and buys that field." Christ himself is the stone of infinite value. It is more important to have a relationship with Christ than to own the whole world. G K Chesterton said, "The Christian faith has not been tried and found wanting, it has just not been fully tried." As Tolstoy said, "Everyone thinks of changing the world, but no one thinks of changing himself." Christ calls us to himself so that he might forgive us and bring healing and blessing into our lives. He then becomes to us of infinite value. Jesus called the disciples so that they would be with him and that he could send them out to preach. (Mark 3:14)

Belonging to Christ and spending time with him develops the most precious of relationships. Christ then commands us to go in his name. (Matthew 28:19) Communion leads to communication. William Faber, founder of the London Oratory, has said, "Love's secret is always to be doing things for God, and not to mind because they are such very little ones."

It is through doing small things well in the name of Christ that our faith grows and matures. Hudson Taylor the nineteenth century missionary needed to learn to trust God in the small things before he could ever have a major impact in China. He learnt to trust God when he was working for a man who frequently forgot to pay his wages. Taylor began to pray that the Lord would provide his food. As he did so, God gave him all he needed, often in miraculous ways. This early lesson proved invaluable when he reached China.

On his first visit there he was in a sailing boat and very close to the shore of islands where there were cannibals waiting. The ship had no wind and was drifting towards them. The captain came to Hudson Taylor and asked him to pray. "I will pray," said Taylor, "provided you set your sails to catch the breeze." The captain said he would not make himself a laughing stock by putting them up whilst there was a dead calm. Taylor replied, "I will not undertake to pray for the vessel unless you will prepare the sails." And so the captain relented and the sails were hoisted. While he was still praying, someone knocked on Taylor's door. He asked, "Who is there?" The captain's voice replied. "Are you still praying for the wind?" "Yes," replied Taylor. "Well," said the captain, "You can stop praying. We have more wind than we can manage."

When we give our all to God and offer to take up the cross each day and follow him, we are saying, "I am setting my sails to catch the wind of heaven." We are saying, "Here is my sail, Lord. Be the wind in my sail so I can be the best that I can be for you and your kingdom here on earth."

My desire, as I close this book, is that each one who reads it might have a better understanding of suffering and pain. As Raymond Lull said, "The more you understand, the better you can believe." Having believed, may we catch the wind of the Holy Spirit so we can be effective in bringing the love and life of God into every corner of this world.

Bibliography

—ɯ—

Chapter 1

Harold Lamb. Alexander of Macedon: the journey to the world's end.

The Mental Health Foundation report. The Big Picture. 1999

Ernie Kish. Blue institution. Bertram's print on demand. 2001

Chapter 2

Martin Buber. I and Thou. Translated by Ronald Gregor Smith. Scribner, 1958

C S Lewis. The four loves.

Chapter 3

Jane Austen. Pride and prejudice.

Edward Gibbon. The history of the decline and fall of the Roman Empire.

Chapter 4

Henry Parry Lidden. Lidden's Baptist Lectures 1866

Roger Forster and Paul Marston. God's strategy in human history. 1989

Chapter 5

C S Lewis. The lion, the witch and the wardrobe.

Chapter 6

William Golding. The lord of the flies. 1954

Web site referred to

Transformation videos: sentinelgroup.org/videos.asp

Lightning Source UK Ltd.
Milton Keynes UK
25 February 2011
168206UK00001B/2/A